I Am a Queer & I Talk to Bees
Introducing Witchy Me

Ashley W. A. Crowell

Edited by: Amanda Young

Publishing House
Windy April Healing Services LLC
St. Louis, Missouri

Copyright © 2019 by **Ashley W. A. Crowell**

All rights reserved. No part of this publication may be reproduced, distributed or transmitted in any form or by any means, without prior written permission.

Windy April Healing Services LLC
PO Box 8369
St. Louis, MO 63132
www.ashleywacrowell.com

Book Layout © 2017 BookDesignTemplates.com

I am a Queer & I talk to Bees: Introducing Witchy Me / Ashley W. A. Crowell -- 1st ed.
ISBN 978-1-7342727-0-3

For my Beloved Family

Contents

Regarding Me 1

When I asked the Right Question 5

My Mommy Dearest 9

That time I faced my own mortality 17

My Bro 21

Why I don't like my birthday 27

The Shock and Aftermath 37

And the Defenses Went Up – and stayed there. 45

Did I Mention I'm a Queer? 53

When I heard the Call 65

When the Radical Wiccan Came to See Me 69

That time I coined a new term to explain my darkest days 75

Those years I did a lot of drugs 81

That Time I Self-Mutilated... and lost all my friends ... 91

That time I had myself a nervous breakdown 99

When I gave Birth a Couple of Times 109

That Time I Lived like a Missionary in a Third world country on American soil 121

The Florida Times 129

My Weight Loss Journey 135

Surviving 147

When my Gifts Showed Up...157

A Chapter of Channeled Writing for You 167

The Feud between Mom and Cheri 173

Collective Energy Deterioration Theory 179

The Jesus Test..185

My Urban Pilgrimage 191

My Question for God 203

About that Appointment 209

Once Gaia Started Speaking to me...............................213

The End of the Introduction 219

Acknowledgements and then some

First off... I have to thank my editor, Amanda. She is the shit. She helped turn my messy yet super interesting story into a book that reads so well... Amanda and I reconnected very recently and we can't even quite figure out exactly how it happened. It was this awesome accident. She is truly a good friend. The universe did me a solid putting our paths back in parallel after having a friendly, yet distant relationship in high school. I am more than lucky to have her in my life.

Next... this is incredibly important. I realize at this point, we hardly know each other. As you get to know me in this book, I want it to be absolutely clear that I am telling these stories from my own point of view. There is stuff in here that shows less than glowing examples of people at their worst. I am speaking about my ex-husbands. I want to make sure that you as the reader understand both of these people went through just as many struggles and trials as me – maybe more so. I ask, respectfully that you leave them the fuck alone. Do not assign anger, do not get offended, do not pursue a quest to obtain their identities. I know it's easy to be an amateur stalker in this world, but these guys don't deserve that. One of them is the father of my kids and we have a great co-parenting relationship. The other... I have zero contact with him on any level including social media. He is probably in a great place in life now. They are both people who experienced some tough days and times. We all fucked up... and we all grew. Please be respectful of their privacy. And save your judgments ... they are not welcome. You will hear me say plenty of choice words, but my words are personal reflections and reactions of some pretty shitty experiences and difficult times... all of which are now in the past. This book is to help propel people forward, so let's extend that courtesy here too.

Please and thank you.

Now... on with the show.

Chapter 1

Regarding Me

I WANT TO BEGIN BY SAYING that every single human I know has been through some shit. I think I could safely say that every human ever has been through some shit. We are all on a journey of conquering self, sorting through karma, and growing to the next level. Each beautiful one of us is dealt a hand that we are meant to have and play... and the real test is what one does with that hand.

I've decided to open the doors to my life in these pages because if we could take measure of all the shit, I think it'd be safe to say that I've earned what amounts to a PH. D from the School of Hard Knocks. I also made it out the other side with wisdom, power, and a gratitude for life that I could not be more grateful for... see what I did there? Ha ha!

As I've come along all this way, it's gotten harder and harder to feel close to people. Most who know me or who have known me in the past probably don't know most of this information. Plus, making new friends has become a task I've almost completely abandoned because there's just too much story to tell. It's too much work.

All anyone craves is to be understood. I feel mostly misunderstood by my family and most of the people I know. I understand myself very well. I am about to take you to outer space with me and show you around my world.

Through a series of amazing events, I have been granted an assembly of spectacular guides in spirit and a very precious 'little birdie' in my ear that are driving forces for my practice as a writer, healer and teacher. I know that there is a reason why I've been given these advisors and my birdie... I want to change the world by helping people.

My experiences have given me a superhuman ability to meet anyone halfway from WHEREVER they are coming from. I am just that seasoned. I am proud of that. I am proud that I love talking to bumble bees in my garden and that they respond with kindness to me. I am also extremely proud to be a Queer living out loud. There is so much to say... this book is an introduction. It's my promise to let the flag of Me wave high as a guidepost for anyone who feels repressed or hidden away. For anyone who feels there is magick looming secretly in their psyche... that needs a voice to explain how to turn it on... how to harness it.

What am I first? A human, I guess, but that is arguable. I Am Me. I've been working for a really long time to uncover and fully step into me. There was so much confusion along the way. I did not always have the right kind of support to help me understand. I am female. I hesitate to stick a label on how I define my 'Queerness', but for educational purposes... I would say that I am a mostly gay man happily parading around in a woman's body. I am a mother because I'm female. I am a parent. I am the Wounded Healer Archetype, having walked the path of pain and suffering in order to receive my gifts. I am a psychic channel. I am a Wiccan Christian magickal yogini monk. I am literally in love with all world religions so I don't like trying to put a label there either. I am an athlete, a singer, a dancer. I love to move and I love to be moved. I find splendor in everything. I converse with all of Creation – including office equipment. I have saved myself so much frustration in my professional life by making lasting friendships with copiers. I have a love / hate relationship with my car because it's really fucking sassy. Most of all? I am so in Love with our Collective Existence. The humans all the way down to those friendly copiers. The plant, animal and insect kingdoms. The mountains, the oceans. The volcanos, the glaciers. The wind and rain. The rainforests and deserts. All I want is to watch our Collective evolve into peace and abundance. I hold this hope so dear that it is my most precious power and toughest burden to bear depending on the day. It is all that matters. It is everything.

This book is not your typical I was born, blah blah blah... these are pivotal moments, stories and experiences that have created me. They brought me here to you, the reader, in this moment so that we may all grow together. I hope you enjoy.

Chapter 2

When I asked the Right Question

I HAVE ALWAYS CONSIDERED MYSELF a graceful person. I've been a dancer for many years, an athlete for most of my life, and a musical theater performer. All of these things require light feet. Now, I regularly have what I like to call 'clumsy days'. These are the days where I cannot for the life of me perform basic functions like walking or talking properly, keeping track of where my keys/phone/glasses are, retaining and remembering basic daily information, etc. Many years ago, I noticed a pattern that the universe kept presenting to me. There was this constant test to my patience that I often made worse by having a tendency to not be on time for things. Now that karmic lesson is another story for another day.

But this patience thing happened everywhere. In the car, in line at the store, with my electronic devices... literally everywhere. It always seemed like the crappier the day, the more severe the delay.

Eventually, I took this constant frustration to meditation to try and find some understanding. An amazing revelation was presented to me in this space. The Divine Voice told me that the most important thing to remember when being tested is to ask myself one thing:

"What am I supposed to be learning right now?"

This revelation literally solved every frustrating, impatient mood I ever had... ever again. It taught me to plan ahead better, to roll with the punches... It taught me to be aware and accepting of synchronicity. It also occurred to me that this question was applicable to literally everything inexplicable that happens in life – especially tragedy.

Now it's important to remember as I begin to dive into the meat here... I will often circle back around to this extremely important point. Why? Because this is what I hope every reader takes away: We can be presented with anything... absolutely ANYTHING in this life. Unspeakable violence, sickness, loss, joyous triumph, lucky happenstance, accidental life altering turns for the better.... Whatever the event, bad OR good... You can still ask this question and more than likely find some wisdom and personal growth in the answer...

"What is the lesson in all of this?"

Chapter 3

My Mommy Dearest

MY MOM IS A PILLAR IN MY STORY... She's been dead for more than half my life, and I have already outlived her by a few years, but her influence on me has been and will continue to be a major contributor to who I Am and why I have turned out this way.

My Mother was a severe abuse survivor. She was sexually and physically abused by her stepfather as a child. I am unsure if my grandma had an awareness of this to be honest, but all parties have passed away so I'll never know that answer. She was also addicted to downers and alcohol for pretty much all of the years I can remember her well.

When Mom was in high school, she was an average student, but an above average reader. I've been told by more than one of my family members and her friends that she always had her nose in a book. She and my Dad met in the 8th grade. They dated late in high school – I am unaware of a lot of the details because I just choose not to ask. My Dad has shared that what he really loved about her was that she didn't throw herself all over him. He was a popular kid and had lots of girls with interest, but my Mom caught his eye. If you've ever seen that movie *Dazed and Confused*, that's a pretty close depiction of the culture they lived in during these years... a really beautiful moment in history

Well they ended up pregnant pretty much right out of high school. After a sweet shotgun wedding for the young lovers, I arrived in mid-April the next year. My Dad said that he felt overjoyed to get to have a family – to be in love and have a baby. My birth story was pretty good considering her young age. She chose to have me naturally – but obviously had some fear because she was in labor for almost an entire day. The doctors insisted that I would arrive before 9:30pm – easily – on the second day. I was born just minutes before.

Fast forward three years, my Dad moved the family to Los Angeles. We stayed back in Missouri until he saved enough money to get us out there. We were reunited in our tiny North Hollywood apartment about six months later. Here was where some of my happiest childhood memories were created, mixed with a healthy dose of why Dad left Mom. Here I experienced my first go 'rounds with police activity because her tendency to become overtly loud and even violent when she and my Dad fought. Once, my Dad spent a night in jail because he punched her. Why you ask? Because she full force hit him over the head with a wine bottle and he punched her back in an angry knee jerk reaction. She was not arrested for starting it despite the head injury he sustained.

I remember once waking up to the noise of their fighting. We had this wooden sliding door that separated our bathroom and bedrooms from the living room and kitchen. I got up out of bed and cracked open the door to a plate crashing against the wall next to my head. SO... I quickly ran back to bed. Mom was a posterchild for someone in suffering. She moved through life like a tornado causing mess, pain and worry to those around her. Those of us nearest to her most of all. My father, Brother and I will forever possess a closeness that cannot be broken because of the shared experience.

When we moved back to St. Louis, my Brother was diagnosed with Leukemia. This was the straw that broke their marriage. My Dad left her, and she never recovered from what went on within their divorce on top of what was happening with my Brother. During the next several years, she bounced around a lot... apartments, family's homes, boyfriend's houses. We did not have a steady place to call home until my Dad bought a house near my school when I was about 12 years old. That's seven years of moving about once a year or more for us kids. We did have a home base at our grandparents' house... that was a safe place for us because it stayed the same, and we spent a lot of time there. They, in fact, still live there today.

The divorce was very messy. Mom was a very unsavory participant. She spoke very badly about my Dad to us, and made us feel both scared and guilty to spend any time with him. She once told me about a dream she had one night,

> "I dreamt that your father and his parents and whole family showed up in our front yard. They were banging on the door and you opened it. They came in and told me they were taking you away, and you and your Brother just went with them. So, after you left, I went to the kitchen sink, grabbed the Draino and started drinking it. Then I woke up."

My Mother committed suicide. That certainly taught me what not to do. Being a survivor of suicide has been a life long journey of finding understanding for someone else's choice. I spent years in a state of anger and guilt trying to understand why. She suffered from Major Depressive Disorder and was probably Bi-Polar. Translation: My mother had very special gifts to offer the world, but she denied them and hid them from the world because she could not figure out how to heal from her childhood trauma. She ran from it by abusing alcohol and drugs and ultimately preferred death to her suffering. I like owning the fact that I am a better version of her that made the right choices to process my trauma.

She also attempted suicide seriously, several times, before she actually succeeded at it. I had to answer the door to police and paramedics more than once because of that. She would get suicidal, call a friend in her horrible state, zonk out on pills and alcohol, then whoever she was talking to would call the cavalry. The 'cavalry' would then come banging down the door to her passed out cold on the couch and my Brother and I sleeping soundly. I remember once feeling terrified because one of the police officers became interrogative to me about what she had taken. He was angry that I didn't know.

He kept asking over and over, and at one point said something to the effect of...

"How can you not know something about what's been going on here?"

I cried. I also developed a severe phobia of police officers for years after that. Having to watch paramedics wheel her out of the house unconscious, and being yelled at by a cop was a little much. I'm not even sure how old I was, but I was younger than 12.

Situations like this really wired me to be fearful. I will briefly cover one extremely ridiculous situation shortly.

The devastating truth of it was that she terrorized so many people in her life with this behavior. People like my Dad, her own family, her best and closest friends, and of course my Brother and myself... all because she was in so much pain from her past and could not bear to address it in any way shape or form. She was unable to find a graceful stride.

Bro and I were lucky... we had friends, school and a pretty great extended family to distract us when she was in a bad way. Generally, for me, productive distraction was always my way of processing the pain. I was really involved in extracurriculars. I played softball and danced; tap, ballet, jazz, pointe. Sometimes I was a bully at school... sadly. The desire for control was not lost on me... and feeling acceptance from others by any means necessary definitely caused me some trouble.

My Mom was a contradiction. The 13 years she was in my life provided me with this insane combination of amazing motherly pearls of wisdom along with scary, depressed, angry and abusive behavior that came from her overwhelming personal suffering.

You know those posters... "Everything I need to know I learned from Kindergarten?" If I made one up about my mother it would be really sad. In all seriousness, she teaches me still every day. I remember because of her that I've overcome both her demons and my own with more grace. I remember to be aware that I am capable of going to a dark place. I also remember that I have chosen for years to live in peace beside this darkness. I harness it to help others and be more understanding of sorrow. Because of my mother, I've developed a strength to walk within the darkest places of human suffering and walk right back out into the light as the situation requires. Her suffering has given me the ability to spirit walk.

Chapter 4

That time I faced my own mortality

AS I MENTIONED, MY MOTHER ATTEMPTED suicide several times before she actually succeeded. It caused me to worry about her a lot. I watched her very closely, and spent some time feeling unsure of my own safety depending on her mood.

Once, a situation that might not have even phased another child, became a really terrifying moment for me.

She was driving us to school one morning, Hardees hash Browns in hand. She perpetually ran late for life (a side effect of depression). So... normal breakfast at home was replaced by drive through breakfast. She was speeding through morning rush hour traffic to drop us off at my grandparents' house. From there, she went to work and we spent a little time watching morning cartoons before it was time to walk to school.

We were driving on a service road beside the highway and traffic was backed up pretty bad. She was cussing a little under her breath, as usual. We stopped in line behind about two dozen cars waiting our turn at a light. Angrily and swiftly, she veered right and got herself into the far-right lane, which was the right turn only lane. Here, she was the first car in line. I was sitting in the front seat, half paying attention to what she was doing. I figured she was going another way to get us to our destination.

I remember noticing that she seemed a little wound up in that moment. She was watching the intersection lights really closely, with both hands on the wheel. When it turned green, she literally floored the gas pedal, jerking me back into my seat.

I looked up, and saw that we were speeding directly towards one of the huge metal posts that held the traffic lights. My heart sunk. I bore down. Everything went slow motion.

My fear wired brain quickly assessed her actions and my analysis told me that she was running the car into the pole to kill herself, and us too. So many emotions in those seconds came into me. Fear, panic, pain, tears welled... and then at the very last second, she jerked the wheel left almost hopping a curb, veering back into the lane we were traveling for the commute, cutting off the cars in the front of the line.

She did this to avoid waiting behind some cars so she could shave minutes off of the drive. She had no idea that in that moment, I thought she was killing us all.

My Brother in the back seat had no idea either. He could not see what was happening.

It was just me there... Needless to say, I was really glad that she didn't want to kill us. But it's quite sad to admit it was a thought I had because of her behavioral patterns. So... this was life with Mom some of the time.

Chapter 5

My Bro

THE REFLECTIONS I WANT TO SHARE about my Brother are from my point of view. He has been through so much on his journey, and I could never understand it fully. But I was by his side for many years, and I could not be prouder. That being said, there is only so much I am willing to say about my Bro... because he is a private guy. His life is his business. This book is about me.

My Brother and I were atypical siblings from the beginning. We had our moments and years where we would piss each other off, embarrass each other, etc. BUT first and foremost, when it came to ANYTHING important, we had each other's backs. Still do.

Growing up, we went through a lot of change... cities, houses, living situations, parental boyfriends and girlfriends. Things were never really steady for many years.

On top of that, his cancer took a toll on normal childhood – mostly for him but also a bit for me. I saw him go through so much hardship and suffering. I witnessed him get spinal taps. I watched as we were informed every once in a while that children he had become friends with succumbed to their cancer and were now gone. I slept in a bed next to him when he started chemo, and remember waking. He would already be upstairs – he was a better morning person than me as a kid. I would open my eyes to his empty pillow and see all these tufts of his strawberry blonde hair all over the pillow while he was losing it from the treatments. When his hair grew back, it was a completely different color.

It was painful trying to understand why this was happening to him. He seemed fine to me, but then he would be so sick on the bad days. Meanwhile, our parents were falling apart, getting ready to separate.

He had this port that stuck out of his chest. It was where they administered medicine for him. It was a tube that had to just be there, protruding from his body for the duration of his treatment.

I just wanted him to be okay. He and I were close before all this happened... but once he came out of the woods, and was ready to really be a kid again, we were really close. We were just good playmates. We both loved video games, being outside, riding bikes... we were great buddies. Our birthdays were three years and one day apart – He was born April 11th, me April 12th. It was kind of like having a twin that was three years younger than me. We were both adventurers. We walked to and from school together every day - all the way to adolescence. Then our relationship shifted.

Instead of being playmates, we became comrades. It was us against the world. Our Dad's girlfriend at the time was a major hard case and we did not like her. We were compliant... well I was compliant... he was moderately tolerant. No matter what, we covered for each other. We lied for each other. We always kept each other protected from trouble – which sometimes was probably not a good thing, but what can I say... we were loyalists to one another.

My Brother was the one factor in my life that stayed consistent through all the change, trauma and drama. We were always together as we were passed around, household to household... situation to situation.

We really loved our Dad too – but there were some things that only the two of us really understood.

Our family dynamic was solid for a good four or five years while we were in middle school / high school. Dad had his girlfriend, but the three of us were the core. We had this bond that no one else understood.

Once I went off to college it was hard on all of us. I have very fond memories of phone calls... every once in a while, I would get a random phone call from both of them... on the same day. They would both call, 'just to say hey'. Talk awhile about nothing, and eventually at the end of the conversation,

"Hey so have you talked to Cory?"

"Can you please call Dad; he is being a dick."

They would call me when they got into it. It was nice to feel needed by them both. I was only a couple of hours away at Mizzou and came home often, but still missed my family.

It also presented me with this pattern that helped me understand them both better. Throughout the years, I've learned that there is a direct correlation: The happier they are, the less I hear from them. When things go wrong, they call. When things are good – it's quiet. So, we continue now decades later with this interesting ethereal understanding. I don't talk to my Brother as much in adulthood. We've just grown in different directions, and that's okay. Becoming who I am kind of confused the relationship. Plus, marrying and divorcing his friend did not help. He encouraged me to date him, then was against it when it got serious. I wish I would have listened to him, but here I am. Whenever I do see him, it's exactly as it always was. AND... he calls when he really needs me. That's good enough for me. I love my Bro.

.

Chapter 6

Why I don't like my birthday

THE LAST YEAR MOM WAS around for my birthday, Bro and I had a combined party at a local roller rink. I remember it being one of the best birthday parties ever. We combined our birthday parties a lot, but it never put a damper on things. We were used to it, and it was nice to get to have twice the party goers when we started to get older.

So, for the party, we each sent out a set of invites to our own friends. It was a great turnout. We have pictures from that day of Mom holding my first cousin that had been born since us two older kids. My great-grandmother, Granny, was there along with the whole family.

Mom hated having her picture taken, but looked great in the candid photos that were snapped.

Going to the skating rink used to be one of our favorite pastimes as kids. Mom liked it because the rink served beer for the parents and played good music. We liked it because we got to stay for the whole three- or four-hour session and just get lost skating to that music. It was like a gang or a tribe to be out there skating fast, speeding past the younger kids with grace, learning how to master turning foot over foot in reverse, having competitive fun with the games they would play like wipeout and the giant dice game... I was never very good at the limbo, but always still gave it a try.

So, our party was a grand success. We had so much fun being with family and friends. Mom was gone about a month after that.

Now, before I go any further, I want to be clear that all of this chapter happened during the last six weeks of Mom's life. I think. It's hard to remember exactly because number one, it was 22 years ago, and number two, I was traumatized and grief stricken which makes memory fuzzy. So, as I explain, know that all of these events happened between that birthday party, which was probably mid-April, and her actual death on May 31, 1997.

That last month of her life, she was not in good shape. She showed up hammered to one of my softball games.

Now don't get me wrong – I was in a CYC summer league, so there were plenty of passionate and jovial beer drinkers in our bleachers. But generally, that came on slowly with a cohesive effort over the course of nine innings. She arrived about halfway through the game with her aunt... already completely drunk. I did not get a worried sense over it until after the game because I was focused on playing.

Once the game concluded, I observed there was concern over what was going on with her. I am not sure who drove her home, but she came back to my house (the new house my Dad had just purchased with his girlfriend) to check it out.

We had not even moved all the way in yet – my room was still basically empty. I remember standing in this bare room with her... listening to her carry on about how great the game was and so on. Then she got this glassy look and said,

> *"Wow you are just all grown-up... I can't believe you are a teenager and that you are getting boobies now."*

I was mortified that she called attention to that weird place in life where my breasts were developing, but still not much more than these weird knots underneath my nipples.

I suppose I was also nostalgic with her. It was neat becoming a woman. I was proud of myself for being good at what I did, doing well in school, and developing into a grown woman from a kid.

So, it was an awkward goodbye when she was shooed home. The situation in which we lived was quite cool at the time. We had been in an apartment about five blocks away with my Dad. Mom was living with her boyfriend and didn't like having us there overnight because we didn't have our own room. So... once Dad bought the house, he decided to sign the apartment lease over to her which would give her a new space where we already had a room set up for us to spend time with her on a more consistent basis.

Then, at his house, we got new stuff to fill our new rooms. It was a pretty sweet deal... or at least it would have been.

She moved her stuff in, but never really set much up. She had a mattress leaning up against the wall in the hallway that was never used as a bed.

During this same 'birthday period', we had another bummer of a situation. My Brother and I had just come home from school, Dad was there too. Knock at the door and there are the cops, with Mom in the back seat of their cruiser. She was inebriated in some way, and her car had stalled at an intersection nearby. I think she had just run out of gas. She was in bad shape. Instead of making some sort of effort to get her car moved or find help (sorry kids, no cell phones yet at this point in history), she just sat down on the curb next to the car until a police officer happened by. So... Dad got someone to help get her car gassed up and taken home while Mom rested at his house. I remember being in the car with Dad when we got to her car and there was a second cruiser there directing traffic.

This was a fuzzy memory for me – probably because it wasn't a good experience. We didn't see her again for an amount of time now lost upon me. Then... that final Friday... my last memory of her alive... she did something that she had done a few other times before. Every once in a while, she would show up early in the morning to give a dramatic good bye. Why? Because she was, once again, suicidal. So... on one hand we were used to this behavior. Usually, it just meant she was having a bad spell and would come out of it again. On the other hand, we got to spend the next undetermined amount of time worrying about if we would ever see her again.

Well thankfully, we were fairly desensitized to this plight, so when Dad came and woke us up at 6:30 in the morning because she was at the door, we were only mildly confused. We made our way to the door and were met with really heartfelt goodbye hugs and wishes. She gave each of us a huge hug a couple of times. She put her hands on our shoulders, looked at us deeply and said something like,

> "Kids... I'm going away for the weekend so you won't see me for a while. I just wanted to stop by and let you know how very much I love you both. I love you both so much, and I always will."

We would try and ask questions, but she would just divert and say she was going camping, not to worry, she just needed to get away.... Blah, blah, blah. As I said, she had done this before.

So, we knew we would spend the weekend worrying and questioning, but also expecting to see her again next week. Unbeknownst to us, this time she was either more ready or more intent on succeeding.

That weekend, I was performing in a musical at my church, so I was busy with dress rehearsals all day Saturday. My Bro was at home, playing, because he was 10 years old. Dad had driven over to Mom's place because she wasn't answering her phone, and he was going to send us to her house that night for our first sleepover with her. He was also probably just checking up on her because of the weird behavior she had been exhibiting all month. He still had a key, since she had just moved in. There he found her body, with that mattress previously leaned up against the wall toppled over her. The inkling was that while she fell to the ground at the end, she reached out and pulled the mattress over attempting to balance herself. She had been gone for only a matter of hours... enough for it to look traumatic but not be gruesome.

She never even set up a bedroom for herself. She had been sleeping in one of the beds in our room. I think she had been in that apartment for a matter of days or maybe a couple of weeks? However long it was... she had enough alone time to finally lose her battle to her demons.

I once asked Dad about that day on advice from one of my therapists. His words,

"It was and will always be the worst day of my entire life."

This was someone he had known since the late 70's. They were married for 12 years. They brought two children into this world. They saw their only son through two years of chemo together and were finally starting to become friends again after a messy and painful divorce. Then she went and killed herself and had the audacity to name him and blame him in her suicide note. She also named her Aunt.

For reasons beyond my understanding, I was given a copy of her suicide note to keep. It was an interesting thing to have access to her last words. It also helped me understand how much suffering she was experiencing, which was perhaps helpful for me in my own healing.

The note also mentioned us – something to the effect of, "I am so sorry for what this will do to my kids...." I honestly don't know where the note is anymore, and don't care. It was so many years ago. Those words no longer matter.

Anyway, Dad was dealing with cops and coroners. I was occupied at church, but Bro had to be distracted. Luckily, we had these amazing people who lived across the street. They happened to be part of my softball family – one of my coaches, his two daughters, who were on the team, and their amazing Mama. Dad called them in to keep an eye on Bro for the afternoon so he could deal with things.

That night was the opening night of my musical at church. I was playing a twin with one of my closest friends and providing the comic relief for the show... which was a place I landed often in other theatrical endeavors. Once, my director in high school informed me that it was because I was one of the only students with authentic comic timing. To this day, I do not consider myself a humorous person, but I guess maybe I am. Because I'm comfortable with my nerdy-ness.

That night... the musical successfully concluded, ice-cream social followed. My family was not in attendance, just my Dad, I think. I don't remember anyone else being there. I do remember seeing him watching me as I socialized with my friends over our ice cream and making note of his slight change in demeanor. He came over and told me we had to go, and after a brief argument, we were in the car and on our way home. I did not notice how quiet he was because I was riding pretty high on the fun of the day.

When we got home, there were a ton of cars at the house and up and down the street. We came inside and my entire extended family was present, occupying every seat in the living room and standing around. Also, the pastor of my church was present. Still completely clueless, I greeted everyone and went on talking about the performance that night. Dad stopped me and called Bro and I over to him. He put one hand on each of our shoulders, and with tears welling, he told us that our Mom had passed away that day.

This moment in time was a horrible benchmark in my life. When I think back on it, what hurts me the worst is that I lost track of my Brother. I went hysterical crying, and just started rotating through hugging everyone who was there. I don't remember where he was. I don't remember embracing him. I lost him. I guess we were both having an individual reaction to what had happened, but if I could go back and change anything, it would have been to hug him. Maybe I couldn't because I had always felt like guardian and mother to him. Maybe in that moment all I could feel was my role as someone's child.... perhaps being his guardian was too difficult for me to bear in those tears.

After some prayer and some comforting words from my pastor, Dad informed me that my friends were outside. It was about half of my softball team – girls I'd been playing ball with for five years. So, outside I went, and they were gathered on the sidewalk across the street. We all ran to each other, embraced in the middle of the street and I cried some more. We all cried.

I was always considered to be a starlet by people... I was generally pretty good at anything I did. I was near the front of my classes academically, one of the best ball players on my teams. My youth pastor said I needed to be up on a stage or in pictures. I was also a very dutiful young person. I was extremely coachable and impressionable. When I look back on these tough moments – I reflect that generally, my commitment to 'soldiering on' was ever present, even in a complete state of grief and shock. It's nice to own that ability, despite everything. It kept me going through the shittier shit that we'll cover later.

Chapter 7

The Shock and Aftermath

THE DAY AFTER MOM DIED, my church musical still had one more performance. I was told that I did not have to participate if I wasn't up to it. Like I said... I felt absolutely no question in my decision to soldier on. It also sounded way more manageable than being at home with my feelings. I remember that the audience was enormous that night. My entire softball team and their parents were there, my extended family, friends who had heard what was going on. This musical was supposed to be uplifting and humorous – at the curtain call I remember seeing so many crying faces. Lots of pride for the fact that I stuck with it, but also pain for what was happening.

The next week as we prepared for the funeral, my grandfather took Bro and me to a floral shop to purchase a flower arrangement for her casket. He gave us a binder and told us we could pick out anything we wanted. I remember Bro being slightly detached from the selection process. The one I liked the best was really colorful. At her wake and service, I remember being proud of how pretty it was. I stopped to admire it a couple of times during the visitation hours.

I remember not wanting to go back to school. We were forced on advice from school counselors. We were sent in late. Every teacher in every class (I was in Junior High and Bro was in 4th grade) was asked to be aware of the situation and inform all classmates so they were aware of the situation. I was met with what felt like an unending amount of scared, nervous faces. Most people had no idea how to react, what to say, or how to treat me. There were so many awkward moments. There was also an outpouring of support. Kids, this was before the internet existed to the public as it does now. There was no viral post to help people rally and have time to think of their reaction. It was just a bunch of people in my small universe who knew me. I received dozens of sympathy cards with every bit of free space signed by hundreds of people. I received dozens of personal letters and notes from both friends and peers that I did not know very well. It was all they could do. And it was lovely.

Almost No One was able to vocalize to me their sympathies. But it seemed like just about everyone had signed their name with a heartfelt little note in all those cards I received. At home, I would sit in my room and read every inch of those cards over and over again. It was like we could have that painful conversation without the embarrassment of my own tears and their embarrassment of not knowing exactly what to say. How do you speak to someone that had just gone through such an event? Nobody really knew. But they all managed pretty well. Also... I still have every single one of those cards today.

Kids... before you had social media to complicate your social interactions... we were unable to analyze ANYTHING before the fact. We had to just feel through situations in real time without forethought. Similar to social media, we did have alienated moments and isolated runs socially. Now there are just more platforms on which to express and experience. You haven't lost anything. It is my belief that you have gained a way to be supportive and give support by exponential leaps and bounds. I now have friends that live on the other side of the world with whom I interact regularly. We send each other love and support as we feel called to. That's the beauty of it. If you aren't feeling strong enough to, the support shows up in the form of someone who does. If you are having a strong as hell day... you are probably interacting with people because you know on some subconscious level, they need to hear it.

It allows synchronicity to play out in so many more ways than what used to be available to us in these pre-digital age times. I am grateful for that now. But I am also infinitely grateful for my circle back in 1997. It was what I needed and what was meant for me.

Okay, tangent complete. Let's circle back around to being in shock. Part of me felt a numbness at Mom's funeral. I couldn't cry. The space where the service was conducted was standing room only... filled with crying people. My maternal grandma showed up a drunk basket case as she mourned her first born. Everyone around me was crying... but me. It was quite unsettling. I was left feeling like something was wrong with me.

This went on for weeks. It actually went on for a few months before things finally shifted for me. I later learned that this was shock... A common occurrence when dealing with fresh grief.

When I finally came out of shock, I was at a Christian church camp called Windermere out near Lake of the Ozarks. I was attending with my youth group. Her funeral was in the first week of June. This camp was 1-2 months later, somewhere in the middle of summer vacation.

We had been given some free time, and I was alone, on a swing. Everything that had come to pass finally welled up in me. I began crying, and it took a couple hours for it to stop. I spent a fair amount of time there at the swing alone, but realized I would have to go find someone eventually or I'd be missed at the next activity. I made my way through camp, still crying. Tears falling uncontrollably to the point that I could barely see. Once someone I knew finally saw me, they brought me to our Youth Pastor. We went back to my cabin and sat together. I was still crying. He proceeded to talk me through what was happening. This was where I learned about the nature of my grief. That it would never truly go away... just change. He told me that everyone in my life would use this moment as a pillar of wisdom regarding who I truly am. People would either be able to say they knew me before she died or they would say they did not meet me until after. For all of you who knew me before... I hold you in a most cherished regard. After I cried these tears, I felt different. I felt released from who I was.

It was the point in my life where the mask went on. Everything about my own identity from that point was confusing for me until I got far enough into adulthood to really understand things. If you were ever in the wake of that confusion... my sincerest apologies. It was just a grieving kid under there... trying to understand why Mom felt sold on the idea of abandoning me.

But, at the very least – the shock was over and I was able to go forth and conquer. And... conquer I did. Extracurricular activities, any accolade that was worth pursuing... earning letters for my letterman jacket, having a job, being well liked and known to my peers, getting good grades. That became the name of the game. It was one of the few things that made sense to me. Mom always spoke about how important it was to excel in school. She hounded me about my grades – even giving me grief for B's because she knew I was capable of straight A's. Holding to that standard seemed like a logical way to honor her and that was what I did.

I am halfway convinced that I lived out the rest of my entire school career in a modified state of shock... trying to impress someone who wasn't even there. I was also subconsciously obsessed with gaining approval and love from... whoever. Generally, it was a boyfriend that I sought. Right when I needed a mother to tell me not to be an idiot – to focus on myself and what I wanted to be in life, that role became vacant and I desperately wanted to be loved. I partied with my friends as an upperclassman, but was never a crazy party girl... I did have my share stupidity in college as many of us do. Also, a continued state of shock. I followed the rules really hard so I could get away with what I wanted to do… usually it was to drive to Mizzou for an overnight party and some stolen time with a high school sweetheart.

However, what it did not accomplish was to help me discover my true calling. I was creating all these plans that had absolutely nothing to do with what I really wanted. It was always about understanding what happened with Mom. Of course, the entire path did take me through directly to my truth. But it remained confusing, conflicted and pretty lonely most of the time.

They say you become capable of executive level thinking around the age of 24… unless you've experienced trauma. I think I came into my higher brain thought abilities around the age of 29. Not too bad of a delay, but delay all the same. The shock helped protect me from things I was not quite ready to see. I am grateful for that.

My greatest take away from these years is so important, but it is not quite applicable yet. It has taught me exactly how I want to raise my kids. Not having a mother to impart warnings, wisdom and well wishes really changed my outcome… like drastically. Tragically. It was like I got lost at sea. My Dad was there – but he was in grief like me… we were all in suffering and he did his best. There were just some things that he did not know how to say. So… on went the mask. And I stayed there behind it for so many years. To this day – I sometimes STILL have to remind myself not to wear it. To be authentic.

This will not happen for my kids, or any young people that I ever encounter in a teaching capacity. What I needed to hear: That I needed to be focused on what I wanted out of life first, and love would come after... that in adulthood I would find the love I desperately sought in someone through mutual passions and interests... That a significant other was the least important thing to consider in my grief-stricken state... That I needed to love and accept me first. I needed to hear that I should keep my heart, body and mind guarded and protected. I needed someone to show me how to pluck my eyebrows and how to cook. I had to learn all this stuff on my own... some of it was easy enough. Other lessons were extremely messy for my mind, body and spirit. But... I STILL made it. I made it. My young ones will fly so much higher. Thank Goodness.

Chapter 8

And the Defenses Went Up – and stayed there.

I STARTED WORKING AS SOON AS I turned 14. I remember anxiously counting the days to my 14th birthday so that I could apply for a worker's permit and get going in the world already. I worked at a fitness club. I was manning the childcare room and when there weren't any kids, I was wiping down equipment, answering the phones and eventually they trained me to do sales cold calls. It was a great job and I stayed there off and on through my freshman year in college. I also played softball and basketball. I was in an excelled academics club in school and several other clubs/extracurriculars to fill my time. But – there was still too much time in the day.

As I understood things in my wounded state, it was my responsibility to carry on with life no matter what. I kept my chin up, my best foot forward, and didn't dare let anyone know I may or may not have been crumbling inside.

As a student of theater, that was a pretty easy role to portray. I put on a mask – I was an overachiever. I wanted to accomplish as much as possible. So... Student Council, International Thespian Society, National Honor Society, theater department performances. I was involved in two different choirs in school, entered soloist competitions and took private voice lessons. I worked the concession stand at football games and attended the Missouri Fine Arts Academy in 2001 as a dancer. If I liked my class, I would do the optional extra credit. I cared very much about what people thought of me.

Why did I care about what people thought? Because I knew they were watching. After everything that happened with my Mom, and the outpouring of support from my peers and teachers, it kind of created this persona. In my signed yearbooks, I got a lot of notes from people stating how impressed they were with my strength and how amazing I was. I now had to live up to my name. I could not crumble, because I was already such a conqueror in their eyes. So… my depression, my shock, my grief all took a very quiet backseat to my mask. My perfect, fun and happy-go-lucky mask. Of course – I was that person too. But deep down, I was really wounded and it took a lot of energy to ignore/hide that.

What really tripped me up was that I had no real back-up. My support system (also in grief) did not always say the things I needed to hear in order to push me the way I desired to be pushed… the way Mom would have pushed. When I would mention my dreams of going to school in New York to pursue acting and try my hand as a performer, I was met with…

"Ehhhh… you have no idea how talented and lucky you have to be in order to make it there."

Also… my family struggled financially, so I chose softball tryouts over poms because it was less expensive. I chose to not enroll in Drivers Ed like everybody was dying to do because it required an extra couple hundred bucks in school fees to participate. Most of my decisions when it came to my future plans were to make things smooth, non-threatening and low risk for those around me. I truly compromised myself a lot.

My first groups of friends were theater people and to be honest they were absolutely awful to me and any other first and second year students. Like hazing type meanness… which was not necessarily wrong. Of course, my desperate need for acceptance and desire to belong to something left me jumping through hoops and eating it all up left and right to get in their good graces. Being in their good graces was really fun. They were neat people... But it created a pattern that really burned me later in my high school career, as I ended up turning around and treating a lot of really nice and decent people like crap.

Little did anyone know that underneath, I was weeping. I had no idea how to live with myself or what had happened to me besides putting up this persona of strength and power. I needed control and this was definitely how I was able to feel like I had some. This is actually one of the reasons why I like social media. It has allowed me to quietly connect with a lot of said people and I've made an effort to be friendly and supportive in the hopes they might see that I am truly a kind person – even if I did not appear so way back when.

Back to my persona... My theater teacher once told me that many theater people will freeze like a deer in headlights when they are forced to be themselves in front of others. I can definitely see that.

I had a pretty easy go at portraying myself the way that I felt looked the best. Had a letterman jacket full of accomplishments and a class ring. Had a boyfriend in college occasionally, and was always a leader among my peers. The teacher's pet, the smart kid... what other ridiculous stereotypes am I missing?

Inside... at home alone... I wrote letters to Mom. I'd tell her about life, beg to understand why she did what she did. Profess my sadness for the loss of her. I mothered my Brother as much as he would let me. As I previously mentioned, we had a lot of fun and we always stayed really close.

For the next 15 years or so I saw an assortment of psychological professionals and went on/came off a variety of anti-depressants. It was difficult reconciling my picture-perfect persona with that business. I remember one point in college when I was seeing a Mizzou psychologist and was on medicine... As my internal chemistry acclimated to the meds, I found that I became a robot. I wasn't experiencing the depression anymore... BUT I couldn't feel extreme joy – or cry happy tears. I remember asking myself why it had to be so much work to just find joy.

I never did a very good job of considering my true heart's desire for most of my years. I've always served others. I stayed in bad relationships for far too long, played it safe in my life ambitions, and generally let the other guy win as a working professional. There were few and far between moments in time where I was really doing for me.

I am now at a point in my life where I realize that I can love myself, be loved, show love and serve others equally with appropriately placed intentions. For quite some time I looked back on all these as misspent years... I now regard them quite differently.

All the years spent – the time I've been here on this Earth – it has been preparation for what I am doing right now. As I sit here tapping away on my keyboard, listening to Annie Lennox radio on Pandora... I am letting tears run down my face. My tiny, yet burgeoning business is providing me with a slowly growing income along with the reward of doing the work I love the most. I have a second job as a gardener to stay grounded and supplement my income. My family is supportive, my kids have food in their bellies and a fantastic support system. My life is so blessed. I am so blessed. What makes me feel more blessed than ANYTHING else... is that I have the ability to share my experiences. I am the wounded healer. I've walked the path of pain... of anguish. I've overcome a significant amount of trauma and abuse... I get to earn a living now by spiritually advising, teaching and healing people. My pain has become my light. And my light shines so bright that it allows me to help others find theirs too. I don't think there is anything that could make me feel prouder or in love with myself.

I have finally retired my mask for good. It kept me hidden from my identity, my gifts and my life purpose. I think that perhaps all these defenses were a kind of necessary evil. Question: What should one learn from a necessary evil? My answer: In order to conquer darkness, the necessary evil exists to protect, train, and empower through experience. The necessary evils in my life made me a fucking OG. That's original gangster, just in case that acronym expired... Some of my slang is outdated, please be merciful.

Chapter 9

Did I Mention I'm a Queer?

I SUPPOSE IT'S SAFE TO SAY that this book is partially a coming out story. It's really important to me that I am saying this out loud. I am not a traditional factory output definition of a woman. This chapter is not an easy one for me. Well, it's extremely easy to know exactly what to write, but the thought of this information becoming publicly available to many of the people that know me makes me nervous. However, I did not write this book for them. I wrote it for you... the reader who picked this out because you thought it might help or you were curious because of your own path. Beyond my own newly acquired freedom, it is for you that I out myself once and for all.

So, I am going to start by saying that by standard appearances, I look and act like a pretty normal straight or cisgender woman to someone with unrefined 'gaydar'. This fact continues to make living quite confusing at times – because my identity is kind of undercover and difficult to recognize unless I make it a point to flaunt it. I do love penis – but in a couple of different ways. I have always secretly had penis envy… wishing deep down that I had one. I'm also more attracted to the male form and that is my sexual preference.

When I was a kid, my tendencies manifested naturally to the label of tomboy. This was acceptable in society and a great place for me to live, not knowing exactly who I was at that point anyway. I was big into sports and riding bikes all summer. I was the go-to kid to fix your bike chain when it popped off. I led the tree climbs to the branches that made most of the other kids nervous. I blazed the treks through the woods and talked the younger kids into leaping over the creek at that one spot… because it's the best spot to do it. We crossed over downed trees suspended over 20 feet of wooded valleys, we explored any sewers we could fit into… Basically we were running around almost breaking bones everywhere we went. Most of the time I was leading the charge. Thankfully, no bones were broken in all these adventures.

Growing up, we used to go to this live nativity performance at a bible college near my grandparents' house. We hiked through an ancient town, met by Roman guards on horseback who commanded us to head to our town of birth for the census. It was like a walkthrough of Mary and Joseph's journey as the birth of Jesus approached. Before leaving on the walking tour, each person is given a little slip of paper that ultimately gets handed off to the men when we arrive for the census in Bethlehem. The papers were pink and blue. I remember being dressed up in my winter gear, hair in a ponytail and beanie on. The woman passing out papers gave me a little blue slip, to my hearts secret delight!!! I looked down at it and smiled... enjoying that she mistook me for a boy. Before I could read and retain the name on the paper, a family member spoke up...

"No, no she's not a little boy, she's a girl!"

Of course, the woman was super apologetic, and took back the little piece of blue paper in exchange for a pink one. The name on the slip was Esther. I always hated the name Esther after that.

I had a 10-year softball career on a summer league and in high school, a two-year basketball career in middle school. I was a dancer too – I fucking love dancing. But I had a hard time fitting in with other dancers because my brain just wasn't quite female.

Into adulthood – in college I almost broke through. I might have actually dated a woman then had I been unattached to my high school sweetheart. I fell in with really cool girls that were involved at the Women's Center on campus. I participated and performed in the Vagina Monologues my sophomore year. At one point, I was cast in a role of a transgender person in the Mizzou New Play Series. I think the director was trying to tell me something. I worked as a research assistant for one of my psych professors (who also happened to be a lesbian) and one of her grad assistants was also gay. It was like I subconsciously surrounded myself with people that made me feel more comfortable... because I was bearing a secret I still couldn't hear. I was so dense. My fellow researchers came and saw me in this play. Sadly, my complete and utter cluelessness remained intact for years.

I remember once taking a class – Psychology of the Mind. It was a course about brain chemistry. The professor was really neat, though I don't recall her name anymore. One of my favorite units in class was when we covered brain development of unborn babies. This was during a time where the daytime talk shows were just barely starting to cover men who were women and women who were men. The LGBTQIA movement only had four letters. Marriage for the Peoples of the Rainbow was still illegal pretty much everywhere.

I was completely floored by learning how many things happen to the human brain during development. There are so many subtle 'disorders' (a better word would be variations) that can happen to the human mind in utero. On a molecular and cellular level, tiny changes and shifts can occur that cause the fetus to develop completely female in their mind while their body develops male and vice versa. Sometimes it happens halfway, mostly or partially (queer, pansexual), sometimes the variations are extremely pronounced (transgenders that do and don't elect surgical reassignment). However it all happens, it's only a tiny window of understanding into how amazing and unique Every. Single. Human mind really is.

For me? I feel like it's an interesting mix. I think my brain is mostly male – I think of it as a blessing. Because chemically, I am female but I carry my chemistry like a man. Kind of like a best of both worlds scenario. It does cause me some inner conflict here and there, though I am quite grateful for my masculinity.

In the workforce, I was always hell bent on being able to physically perform my job just as well as a man – with no assistance. I worked in the restaurant industry and at that time, I used to do push-ups AND one-handed push-ups every day because I'd be damned if I needed to ask for a guy's help to change a keg or take out a heavy bag of linens.

I was also completely ruthless to a man's un-chivalrous advances at the club or wherever I happened to be. In a group of friends, I was the bodyguard – the security detail. I was the one to take it a step further than a dirty look and either turn and face a guy with some choice words or even physically push their ass away from my friends or myself... Like some sort of weirdo with something to prove, but I didn't know what... you could probably call it a slight Napoleon complex...

I felt like my masculinity also helped me to carry my pregnancies, labors and deliveries with more strength. I'll tell those fabulous stories a little later.

So, I floated along in life. All my love affairs were male. I experimented with women, and it was delightful. But, in my heart I knew I did not crave a relationship with a female. When I considered it, I felt like I wouldn't be happy. I really do like penises better. Equally, I love being cuddled and nurtured the way a woman cuddles and nurtures. It's a tall order I suppose.

Wanted: A beautiful specimen that is feminine / masculine minded (any sort of mixture that's going to compliment my own), masculine and male on the outside and ready to be big OR little spoon depending on my mood. Must understand my unique chemistry and be willing to comply because sometimes I want to be in charge and other times I want to be babied. In exchange, I pledge to be able to read your mind and treat you as you've always dreamed of being treated. Or at least do my best. You crazy bitch.

SEE. This isn't easy... we are already arguing.

Anyway... while happily cohabitating with Toby (my second ex-husband) I found myself craving motherhood like a crackhead... Craving motherhood as a queer was an interesting contradiction. Often, as I was discovering and trying to understand my identity, I found myself analyzing this piece of the story. Did it make me not queer? Did it void my queerness? Thing is, I will never escape the fact that chemically, I am female. It's just part of who I am. And that's more than okay.

When my first child arrived on Earth, my truth FINALLY started to become clear. My queer truth. I belonged to support communities on Facebook – I talked to other Moms, nurses, my pediatrician – pretty much anyone who wanted to talk about their experiences in motherhood because above all else, I craved to learn... knowledge is my soul food. Across the board... when I would come back to my own cute little home.... My space where I was the chief and my child was my little tribe... I didn't feel like I was in the same category as pretty much every Mom I spoke to. I had this detachment to my son right from the start. I didn't feel this motherly possession of him.

It scared me because I didn't know what was healthy to feel. Of course, healing from childbirth physically and psychologically is an intense period and must be processed with gentle strength. But even as I found my strength again, I felt different. Different than a 'woman'.

How I saw it – I had this beautiful, magickal miniature human in my arms. I grew him in my womb. I nurtured him with my body and kept him safe as he prepared to arrive in this world. Once he was here... I could see right away that he was not mine. He was a person – an infinite and tiny person that had just arrived from the stars somewhere. He looked around with these eyes in awe of everything he saw. He smiled at my face and laughed at my silly sounds. He understood my words and thoughts and moods. He drank from my body and liked to fall asleep latched for comfort. Our bond was the most beautiful thing I had ever experienced.

But deep down – I knew something with all of my soul. This tiny amazing being was not mine. Within him – there was already written a story. He was going to choose a life for himself – make mistakes, conquer battles, acquire victories that would have absolutely nothing to do with me. I was just here to support him to that point.

I am his teacher, his guide, his coach, his best friend... and then when he is ready, he will disappear from my presence to find himself.

And that made me feel a pride unmatched by any other feeling I have Ever. Had. I looked forward to watching it happen. I didn't feel sadness over losing him. I didn't feel possessive of him. I didn't weep for what I would lose when he grew up. I celebrated the notion. I felt a pride for it. I still do.

When he took his first steps at daycare instead of at home with me, I did not feel upset. I felt excited that he started walking! As he grew out of his baby clothes and his baby face into the look of a small child, I saw who he was becoming and rejoiced. I did not cry tears for losing my baby – watching him grow into a person was so beautiful to me. There were little pangs of sadness here and there... but nothing like the lamented nostalgia I have always observed from other Moms.

Tell me... does this sound like the inner dialogue of a Mother or a Father?

So, all of the sudden I had this panic. What did this mean? What was I? What the fuck was I? I would have the discussion with Toby to try and talk it out in an attempt to understand myself and not spiral into a confused state. Once again, I was a new Mom which is a delicate place to be. He would get frustrated and annoyed with me. He'd ask why I had to put a label on it... why couldn't I just be whatever I am and not worry over the details of actually understanding my identity?

Well that just wasn't good enough for me. I needed to understand myself. I also needed a spouse who supported that desire. He didn't mean to fall short. He was allowed to feel how he felt. I do believe my journey to my truth might have left him feeling insecure in regards to what that meant about who he was. An unfortunate, yet inevitable side effect. Definitely a reason why we slowly grew apart.

Toby once told me that he was uncomfortable having sex with me because I looked too much like my Brother 'sometimes'. That was a compliment and a gut punch at the same time for me during self-discovery. In my heart of hearts, I liked that he thought I looked like my male Brother. But hearing him confess his dislike of me was so painful. I developed this idea that my masculinity was unattractive... like I needed to just look female and feminine and own that without embracing androgyny in order to be accepted by my partner.

It was quite a conflicted place to live. While I felt in my heart that my brain and my wiring was just plain different... I also really did, and still do enjoy being a female. I find my body to be artful and exquisite. I wouldn't want to trade it for anything. I love my femininity and I also love my masculinity.

As I mentioned before, I still possess a desire to be caressed like the woman I am. It's a strange and interesting place to exist. I cycle and experience chemical mood swings from said cycles. I am governed by the moon. But I am also really good at video games and geometry (both are known to be strengths of boys, not girls). I like to train beside men because I can match their strength. I make friends with males more easily. I've always related to them better, felt more comfortable with them.

I've grown to love myself very much. I know that my partner will love me just as much... especially in a day and age where this kind of honesty is becoming valued instead of hidden.

How do I express myself? I talk about who I am when I feel comfortable. I've got an undercut that reaches from the back of my head around to above my right ear. I've got a tragus piercing and a single small gauged earring in what was always known as the 'queer' or 'gay' ear... just to prove a point. But – it's a double piercing so I can put in a cute pair of chandelier earrings when I'm expressing femininity. I can wear my hair down in curls and look straight. Or I wear it up in a high pony tail or messy bun to show off my undercut and let my queer flag fly. I've had my stylist shave designs in the side/undercut when feeling fancy. And I change the color to something loud when I'm feeling kicky. Why? Because I've decided to proudly and unapologetically live out loud. As a healer, as a queer, as a conqueror of life. Come join me you quiet conquerors in waiting. I know you are out there.

Please, please... live in honesty as well as you can – even if it's in secret. Eventually you will find the person that wants to share life with you - The You of Yous. Those who have endured through this struggle in quiet OR out loud truly will be rewarded with the right partner. I know this to be true for all of us. Have patience and work hard to love yourself fully until they arrive. Be ready to be your best self for them.

Chapter 10

When I heard the Call

THERE WERE TWO PIVOTOL POINTS which occurred in my childhood that materialized my personal call to serve others spiritually.

When I started watching musicals, I. Was. OBSESSED. I was watching them non-stop and loved the worlds created within the story. The first musical I ever saw was *West Side Story*. Still one of my favorites to this day. Well around the age of 11 or so, my grandparents went ahead and let me pop in their VHS copy of *Jesus Christ Superstar*. Ahhh, the rock opera that embodied the Son of God's Work. My grandpa loves to tell the story of when I first watched this musical all the way through.

He always remarks that the further into the movie I got, the closer I scooted to the television. At the end of the movie – when they are sounding the noises of his actual crucifixion, they snuck into the den where I was watching and observed me kneeling right in front of the TV. My head was bowed into my hands and I was sobbing loudly into them. I remember feeling so deeply moved by the story. By His sacrifice and the injustice that lead up to his Earthly death.

At other points in childhood, I watched stories of Jesus' life on VHS cartoon video tapes. They were animated versions of many popular bible stories like The Sermon on the Mound, The Prodigal Son, The Good Samaritan, and of course the birth story... dozens of them. My Brother and I watched these tapes a lot and had this romanticized idea of Jesus... and watching JCSS was a real eye opener for me. There was just so much beautiful and genuine emotion. So much real-life struggle. I knew what struggle looked and felt like. Watching the story in this form really touched me.

The other amazing experience I had was within one of my Mother's most lucid moments I can remember during my entire childhood.

She was a devout Catholic. She took us to mass every Sunday that we were with her. The curious thing for me as a child was that she never put us through the bible classes – we never had a first communion – so when it was communion time at mass, my Brother and I had to hang back with the little kids. We must have been about 11 and 7, maybe? After a certain point, it started to cause me embarrassment. So, one day I decided to ask her about it.

> *"Mom – why can't we take communion with you? It's embarrassing to have to sit in the pew while all the regular people go up there. Why didn't you put us in the classes so we really belong to the church?"*

She sat quiet for a moment. Then finally, she said,

> *"Well, Ashley. I don't know if you are a Catholic."*

I responded with silence.

She continued,

> *"When you are old enough... read books, learn about the world, learn about religion, then choose your beliefs based on what works for you."*

It was shocking for me to be so young and be given so much power over my own beliefs. This conversation lit a fire in my soul. I was already an avid reader myself, but became even more so. It had not occurred to me that reading could give me answers about the mysteries of life and the universe. For all her faults... Mom had a consistent sprinkle of these amazing lucid moments... Tidbits of parental wisdom that kept me afloat through the grief of her passing, the years that I missed her presence, especially as a teen and young adult. Of course it did not replace completely what a mother is meant to provide for a young woman in regards to growing up in general... but... I was able to walk with a lot more grace thanks to these little conversations that she shared with me.

Chapter 11

When the Radical Wiccan Came to See Me

I HAVE COME TO UNDERSTAND that my gifts as a psychic channel have been passed down to me by my maternal line. Woman to woman to woman. I had no idea there was anything mystical about me until I was about 16 years old.

It had been a couple of years since anyone in my family had spoken to Mom's Mom. We called her Grandma Cheri, though her name was Charlotte. This was a familial name passed from woman to woman for five generations. After a lot of exploration of this ancestral line, I believe the name had something to do with our role in the burning times, but that is another story for another time or book.

Grandma Cheri came to stay with us at Dad's house for a mini-vacation. She wanted to spend time with us. We did not really know her very well, but always felt a comfort seeing her, as her presence brought us closer to Mom.

One of the nights, she and I were sitting outside in my backyard at the patio table. She was smoking and drinking. I was curious to hear whatever it was she wanted to say. I always looked up to her and was intrigued by her eccentric ways.

She shared with me all kinds of fascinating things. When she drank, she developed an Irish accent. She believed it was because she had been an Irish terrorist in a past life. That was a little out there for me, but fascinating nonetheless. At the time, I was technically a Southern Baptist. I was not attending church regularly anymore as I was in the throes of the 'Angry at God' phase… BUT my roots were still there.

So the former Irish terrorist told me about her powers. She was a palm reader. It was part of her livelihood in Florida. She lived in Fort Lauderdale for years. She told me stories.

"Well you know, your Papa Flip was a Hell's Angel back in the 70's. Once we were hanging out in a bar and I

happened to know someone there. This guy, he and I went to high school together. We caught up, and chatted just for a little while. I was there with your grandpa and he did not like the conversation I was having one bit. Several of his buddies were there with us. He asked me to head on home because they were going to ride. I found out later on that my friend had died that night. More than died – your grandpa and his friends provoked him. They picked a fight and stabbed him to death in the alley outside the bar. No one ever caught them. And he died because I happened to know him.
After that, I told Flip (his nickname) that it was either me or the gang. He left the gang... but we ended up splitting anyway..."

16-year-old me was sitting in shock at the story she had just told. And that was nowhere near the end. She told me that she used to go to Vietnam protests a lot. She was loud about trying to change things. She grumbled that my generation had nothing to fight for. That we were all just meandering around, no cause to believe in, no banner to hold up.

At one of the protests, she was accompanied by my Mom and Aunt. Mom was about two and my Aunt was a baby. This was one of the protests where she was arrested for whatever reason... kids and all. They had her in a holding cell for hours. She wasn't scared, no child services were called.... This was just part of how things worked back then. Amazing. She laughed, saying,

> "I didn't know how long they planned on keeping me, but once your Aunt had a dirty diaper, their decision was made much more quickly. I changed her, and set the diaper out near the front of the cell... They let me free within 15 minutes."

She told me about her psychic ability. I remember feeling nervous and attempting to clear my mind of anything incriminating for a 16-year-old's grandma to know. I didn't know exactly what being psychic meant.

We talked about my Mom. She said that Mom became so angry with her once she was an adult. But before that... as a teen... Mom would bring people home to Grandma Cheri for help. She would worry about friends at school going through stuff. She would see people in pain or scared or confused, and would bring them to her Wiccan mother for comfort and counsel. She had this sense that the work my grandma was doing meant something. I have no idea where the fracture occurred between them... I'm sure it had something to do with the abuse and trauma from one of the stepdads – but that doesn't really matter anymore. They are both gone.

So... the Wiccan grandma told me that our gifts... our powers... were a very present thing for us.... the women in our family. She said that since my Mother was gone, 'it was now up to me'. She didn't explain the nature of the gifts or how they would coalesce for me.

The most important thing that I took away from this interesting backyard conversation was about humanity. She was talking to me about our species – how awful it was (she was so jaded). She told me that everything was connected and that when we die, the place where our souls communicate is called the 'Collective Energy'. She also said that it was in horrible shape because of the state of our species overall. There were a lot of gloom and doom overtones to the calling she spoke of – whatever duties that were now 'up to me'. I did not particularly like this about her. It left me feeling sad. There was this detachment from joy within her. Like something had taken her heart and it never returned... and for whatever reason, she never went looking for it.

What was up to me? It sounded a lot like crazy talk. Of course, as a teenager, I was already in a state of temporary insanity that could not be helped. I took this statement with a grain of salt and a dash of worry. It laid dormant in my psyche for years, and came flooding back when I finally awoke to my gifts. We'll cover this in another chapter, I promise.

So... Grandma Cheri, my Radical Wiccan maternal grandmother... she remained a presence in my life that sparked mystery and wonder.

Before all the weird conversation, she was quietly showing me her Wiccan practice. When I was three years old, she began bringing crystals to me and hanging them in my window. I am sad to say that most of them have been lost over the years. But one has remained. It hangs in my office on this very day.

She would talk to me about how magickal and special they are. That, when placed in the sunlight, they would tell secrets to me.

Every interaction with her was quite interesting. She was truly unique. Simultaneously she was that jaded person… she drank a WHOLE lot and was not necessarily the easiest woman to get along with. Once, we visited her in Florida. I remember observing her ordering vodka on the rocks at the beach bar in the middle of Fort Lauderdale summer heat… How? I hate day drinking in the heat unless it's a yummy refreshing frou-frou something or other. I only saw her about a half dozen times in the last several years of her life… eventually she became angry that I did not make enough of an effort to visit her and essentially disowned me. She died angry with me.

I am very proud to report that it has no bearing on my current relationship with her. We are now very close and I am able to call her for council or comfort whenever needed. I am a lucky witch.

Chapter 12

That time I coined a new term to explain my darkest days

WHEN WE DID THOSE FUTURE career assessments in Junior High, the results for me were really confusing and disappointing. In honesty, I am not sure what I wanted the results to say, but for better or worse, I was assigned the following: It was suggested to me that I either become a professional athletic trainer or coach, or join the military.

One of my most recent jobs was a professional kickboxing coach (I was the manager, but I also coached and it was my favorite part). Such irony... That in all the madness of the twists and turns in my life, I ended up exactly where the assessment said I would be. I'm also working on my entrance exams for the Air Guard currently because it's the only branch that will accept me at my ripe old age. The benefits are just so good and it feels like a safe bet for me as far as retirement goes since owning a small business is so bumpy in the beginning. I'm in a bit of panic in regards to making sure I can provide the best life possible for my kids these days.

When I was young, I liked the idea of joining the military – the discipline it would teach me, the perks, tuition assistance, and belonging to a cause. It all sounded really awesome – especially to a blossoming, yet unaware queer like me. It was a secret I kept through junior high and high school. The problem? 9/11.

The towers fell the same year I would be speaking to recruiters. It would have landed me right into the heart of that war. I probably would have ended up with a bad hand in all that – perhaps death or severe injury... Logically, my family shut me down right away.

Why did they shut me down? Because they were afraid for my safety and wellbeing. It was from a place of love and I understand this. I wish very much that I had not listened. I wish that I would have followed my heart and my dreams so many times back then.

But, I listened... and did not ever join the military. We all know what a war veteran is. When they choose to wear their hat or jacket or vest, we can see immediately that this is a person who potentially experienced harsh, terrifying and psychologically traumatic events. Anyone who has ever been in the service or a first responder of any kind can relate to the following:

Imagine the inner dialogue on any given day:

"I'm afraid for my life. But I chose this. I might die. But it's for the greater good. I might be damaged forever. But I chose this. I am facing life or death situations every day. But I chose this. I barely see my family and may never see them again. But it's for the greater good."

This... is what causes psychological fracture and trauma for someone who chooses to be a first responder or service person.

Now imagine that instead of a war, the subject matter is the darkest types of human conditions. Homes where there is neglect, abuse, and fearful situations for the young people OR the adults in the house. The survivors of these types of stories are also veterans.

My dear Karma, like I said – she is a tricky bitch. When I was still pretty raw from my darkest life experiences, I journaled a lot. During those times I put a lot of pain and psychological anguish into those journal pages. I used to try and justify all the unfortunate events of my life... and landed on a term that I coined. It was an invention that I thought I might someday use to describe what it is to be a severe trauma survivor.

Psychological War Veteran.

I felt this term perfectly reflected my own situation. While I never joined the military, and may or may not go through with joining the Air Guard... I still consider myself a veteran of sorts. What I endured amounts to internal war. It was struggle inflicted upon me without my permission.

Playing the devil's advocate... I would argue against my own point and say that on a soul level, I absolutely did sign up for all this before I was born. I realize that the Divine would never give me more than I could handle. Truth be told, I can see myself out there in the ethers somewhere pre-conception – raising my hand to volunteer for a bunch of the toughest shit – because all the other souls in the room had these faces that just screamed, *"Please. No. Don't make me do that."* So, I looked around and volunteered to take the bullets... to walk in the darkness. I knew I could do it.

BUT... as a little kid growing up that wisdom was not within me just yet. It took years of searching, reflecting, healing and resetting in order to come to terms with the stories from my darkest years.

When I write about these times... it is draining. It makes me tired. I have to tell myself that I am no longer that person. My mantra is: These things happened long ago and I am not that person anymore. These stories are from then and I am me now.

It's difficult to admit that it's still hard to visit those places, and in fact at some points when writing this book I had to put it away temporarily because reliving the stories triggered old pain.

What was meant to happen to me happened regardless of battlefield location. I was meant to endure some fucked up shit – and instead of seeing action as a soldier, I was sent through a gauntlet of psychological warfare in the form of sexual, verbal and physical abuse, major depression and anxiety, subsequent drug dependency, self-mutilation and alienation from loved ones. Instead of wearing the injuries sustained on the outside in the form of physical disability... my wounds were inflicted to my insides – to my heart, soul and mind.

To top it all off, I do not wear a hat or vest or jacket that denotes my status as a Psychological War Veteran. I hold it silently, without a banner. Until now anyway. Now, anyone who reads this book will understand a lot about me. With all of my heart, I hope that it provides proof that we are capable of overcoming anything. To anyone who has ever suffered: You are not alone.

So boom everybody. Karma happens in whatever form. It always finds you. As I write, we are in a month of mental health awareness. It is truly an invisible weight. No one struggling with their mental health enjoys having to explain. And yet – in order to be truly understood and loved, we kind of have to.

Remember with mercy please... that there are millions of people who suffer silently... every day. Welcome now to my darkest days.

Chapter 13

Those years I did a lot of drugs

(Warning: This chapter has explicit content. Please be aware and read with caution if sexual abuse or heavy drug language is a trigger for you.)

THIS WILL NOT BE EASY for me to write. These years were the darkest for me. I came close to death. Not because of overdose – because of the path I was on. It was leading to untimely death. My first ex-husband, let's call him Jethro. Jethro really knew how to make me feel safe in this dark way.

He had an obsession with dark forces. He listened to dark music. He loved the numbers 666 – for their devilish stigma. He was very intelligent. He paid attention to current events. He lied to me a lot. He was an addict when I met him – had been for years, and coaxed me into drug use with him in such a gentle way... I felt like I was sold a car that I didn't need, but couldn't help myself. When he asked me out and took me on a date he did all the things a girl wants... He was polite, sweet and confident. He opened doors for me and he had quite a handsome smile when he looked at me. I liked seeing how much he liked me on his face. On our second date... he handed me a pill and talked me into taking it. I was so goddamn naïve. I had never gone through an 'experiment with drugs' phase...though I certainly wanted to. I was a young adult, out of college, single. He was so suave (probably from drug induced confidence). It was very enticing to be treated with such a curious influence. I was interested.

That pill he gave me kept us up all night doing a lot of really fun unmentionable things. It was a methadone pill. SO... our second date this man gave me a small dose of pharmaceutical heroin and I went along with it – not knowing what methadone was. This was a period in my life where I truly wish my mother had been around to slap me upside my head and say, *"What the fuck are you doing?*

Get away from this guy!" I felt this was something that everyone in my family was thinking, and I am sometimes hurt that no one ever had the gumption to get into it with me during this early period.

Anyway, that was about all I saw of the drugs until he hooked me in with the fun hallucinogens. That was an absolute blast. We had these drug induced experiences together... which were amazing. I am not against hallucinogens... humans have been experimenting with altered states of consciousness for thousands of years and they do have their place.

But eventually, he started bringing me over to a certain friend's house and asking me permission to snort drugs that were too far out there for me. He was always insistent that I didn't have to try it, though he always offered gently.

It occurred to me in retrospect that what he was trying to accomplish deep down was a desensitization. He got me super-duper comfortable with his own addiction, introduced it to me slowly and gently... even asked me permission for him to use... which what the fuck? Then he coaxed me up close to it... helping me to make friends with it. Eventually my innocent and stupid naïve tendency gave way to enough curiosity to try it. Why? Well this guy was quite a gentleman. He showered me with compliments and affection. I loved the attention. This was the way I wanted to be treated. It was the first time I'd been treated so well by a man. I am so disappointed that the very first one with the right kind of manners also happened to be an addict. My idiotic self thought... *"How bad could it be?"* I tried it and of course it was amazing. Within a matter of months I had developed a dependency. So now – he had me. It was like I was captured and pulled into a pit to live with him. A place where he could feel justified in his darkness because he has a beautiful woman next to him who approved... Who was stuck in the throes of it too.

The dependency for me lasted about four years. Near the end as I watched every bit of disposable income being sunk into drugs, as I saw brushes with the police circle closer and closer, as the bill money started getting spent on it... I became so sick of the rat race. I became so ashamed of myself.

Of course using so many hard drugs regularly did not do me any favors either. It led to deeper dependency, which led to experimenting with stronger drugs... cutting the drugs with harder drugs, adding more drugs to the drugs for a higher high. I could go on...

I could spend a couple chapters talking about the time that I smoked crack that was cut too strong and it left me strung out on a bed all night shaking and sweating. I could talk about how he would mix up these speed ball concoctions (heroin and cocaine) so we could feel good and stay up late at the same time. I could talk about how in the time I was with him, I attended several funerals of his close friends who died from the very same drugs we were doing. I could list all the jobs I quit or lost because of the darkness. I could also go into how badly I alienated my friends and family by showing up to life on drugs, and how much I wished deep down for somebody, anybody to pull me aside and scream at me about what was going on. That much detail might be entertaining to some... or it might just be a little too shameful for me to write and painful for you to read.

I don't feel it's necessary. I think these situations scarred and hurt my friends, family and myself quite enough.

The toughest part was finally getting away. This guy was quite a controlling force. He would call me at work when I was a waitress to ask me how much I thought I would make so he knew the quantity of drugs he could buy that night.

On one hand, he made me feel like a Goddess. He would step into the shower when I was in there and insist on washing my body for me. He was a tender lover some days. He continuously reminded me of how protected I was. He kept control – a kind of love disguised slavery.

On the other hand... he threatened to kill me if I ever cheated on him. He explained in very specific detail how he would actually kill me (poison or a knife to the throat), how he would dispose of my body (electric carver, meat grinder and feeding my meat remains to the stray animals of our south city neighborhood), and how he would hide the information from my family (fake travel plans, suitcase packed/missing and note from Ashley saying she's running away).

He also liked to have sex with me when I was unconscious. Once he violated my 'back door' while I was passed out drunk. It was the first time that sort of sex act had ever been done to me. The next morning he reported the information with this boyish smile on his face as if I was supposed to be turned on and feel complimented by what he had done. I was disgusted, but also felt trapped because I was on vacation with him at the time.

Otherwise, he mostly would insert in the usual manner when I was in a deep sleep and probably high from the H. It was an act that told me he enjoyed owning my body with or without my presence. He used it how he pleased without my permission as his wife in such a way that I wouldn't and/or couldn't put up a fight. I would wake with my face in my pillow to him taking me from behind, holding me steady because I was limp from being asleep. I was told years later that there is a technical term for such a thing... 'Marital rape'.

He liked to play rough when I was awake - choking, hair pulling and slapping. Once I asked him to choke me hard. I was trying to get him to squeeze hard enough so I would pass out... to not be present. I literally wanted to be unconscious. I remember closing my eyes and trying to drift off while he moved his body and held his hand on my throat. All of the sudden, he quickly pulled his hand away. I opened my eyes and saw this puppy dog pain in his face. It was like he could see that he had fundamentally broken me in some way.

Now a lot of this kind of behavior is considered regular kink in a HEALTHY relationship. There are happy couples out there that enjoy being weird in all sorts of ways. I've always considered myself to have a very healthy and vibrant sexuality. I guess that's why I let it all happen. In a healthy relationship where there is intimacy not based in darkness, go crazy. But this was not healthy. Everything between us was perverted by the darkness he brought with him in the beginning.

Most of it was probably because of the drugs. He's sober now as far as I know. I finally sent him away from my life when I caught him using needles.

Let me be clear when I say – I never in my life used needles. Ever. I would always snort the drugs we did.

Once I caught him with the needles, I confronted him, and was met with,

> "Please, Ashley, just let me do it to you once so you can see it's not that bad."

That was the end for me. At that point, I was already not using much anymore. I was still paying for his habit because he insisted that he was weaning himself off slowly but surely (again). I was at a point where I might have a bump here or there maybe once or twice a week, but I had broken my dependency... the bump was to self-medicate and create a fake tolerance for watching his sickening behavior continue after several trips to rehab.

I was just so scared to kick him out. I was afraid anything drastic would make him snap and I'd eventually get a taste of the insanity that was previously threatened for bad behavior.

Nevertheless, the needles were the line for me. So... I talked him into moving out and staying with a family member to give me some space and time to think. I insisted that I still wanted to be with him to lessen the blow, though deep down I was so very done. I was ready to bury this fucker and dance on his figurative grave. But... I chose to be extremely tactful because of his controlling nature. Thankfully, it worked.

I got him out of the house, and of course, enter into the picture of Ashley's already screwed up life: future ex-husband number two.... We'll call him Toby and get into him later.

For now, it's important for me to say that I made it out of my drug dependency and the relationship that fostered my darkness. The divorce was drawn out and just plain awful. His presence in my life haunted me for years afterward.

This mother fucker had such a hold on my soul – took so much from me that he somehow had an awareness of the exact worst time to call me. The day I found out I was pregnant with my first born son – he called. He didn't know that I was pregnant, he just happened to call that day because he needed paperwork from me.

Two weeks before my son was due – he called. He had found sobriety and was reaching out to work his steps... but I was pregnant, fragile and somehow on some level, he was still able to haunt me and tap into my fragility even from so far away. He wanted to take me to lunch to apologize and make amends.

I told him,

> *"I am happy for you and glad you've found sobriety. I wish you all the best in the world, but the best thing you can do for me is lose my fucking number and never call me again."*

He told me he could do that, and he did. But his mother... his fucking mother for years afterward kept giving my number to her creditors and lawyers or whoever as a reference so they would call me looking for her. It happened so much that I ended up having to change my number so it would stop triggering me.

    Let's end this one with... Good Fucking Riddance.

Chapter 14

That Time I Self-Mutilated... and lost all my friends

CONTINUING WITH OUR TOUR through my darkest times... I'm still on Jethro – this fucking winner. He was in rehab... again. I had moved into a spare room with a friend that I had known for over 10 years. We were very close in high school, roommates for a time in college, and just overall really close... well we had been in years past. She and her new husband were allowing me to stay with them while I figured things out with the druggie hubby, but in all honesty, I was also in bad shape. I wasn't using the hard drugs, but I was still feeling the pains of the habit I had formed, so I was self-medicating with marijuana, muscle relaxers to sleep at night, and barbiturates because I had an insane amount of anxiety over all of it. I didn't actually have any marijuana to smoke – I was actually taking one-hits of weed resin out of a metal socket piece from a socket wrench. If you are street, or hood in anyway, you probably have at least a vague familiarity with what I am saying. If not, you are probably reading this with your mouth hanging open in surprised disgust.

My friend's husband was paranoid like a cop – I think at one point he actually was a cop or highway patrolman or something... so I'm fairly certain he had gone through my things and discovered the socket. He assumed it was meth... which is really ironic because meth is one of the very few hard drugs I have never tried.

Let's reverse... A short time before this, my druggie hubby and I managed to basically ruin their wedding. It happened under my nose initially, then I was a party to it simply because I was under the control of this really fucked up situation (on account of his addiction)... letting it happen every day. When we were at the groom's parents' house for the rehearsal dinner, my loving husband rooted through their medicine cabinets and found all sorts of goodies in the form of whatever the fuck kind of feel good pharmaceuticals he enjoyed using. He came up to me about halfway through the evening and said that we needed to leave... *"right now"*. I was pissed, I put up a fight, stating that I wanted to spend time with my friends and enjoy the evening. Then I noticed that he started exhibiting the signs of being extremely fucked up. Like he was altered... heavily. So, we left.

He was in and out of happy consciousness the whole way home. He told me with slurred speech what he had done. He showed me the giant pockets full of pills he had swiped from the medicine cabinets of these unsuspecting people who probably needed them. I yelled a lot. I drove angrily. That night, we were supposed to be making a French breakfast set up for the morning because it was our gift to the bride. We were going to make a bunch of cute little items like petit fours and set them up at her house while everyone got ready for the wedding.

Well, he was in this disgustingly altered state, and we ended up getting little to no sleep making all this shit. At the time... I was so skinny – drug girl skinny. We showed up late, he set everything up in a cold sweat, and I got ready alone and embarrassed in a corner of the house. Since he was already there, he insisted that he get to stick around and tag along with the wedding party. He couldn't give me one fucking half day away to be present with my friends.

Here's the icing on the ridiculous cake: On our way out to the site for the wedding photos, he was following the limo that was driving us. The driver called back to let us know that he was swerving on the highway – almost running off the road more than once. Why? Because this mother fucker was popping those stolen pills and was a fucking altered mess back there. He had no self-control. So, we had to pull over on the fucking highway, let me out of the limo, and I had to walk back to him in my beautiful silver bridesmaid dress so I could drive the car the rest of the way and he could pass out in the passenger seat. Not a proud moment.

The wedding party and the bride made up my very best friends at the time. This situation pretty much cost me all of them. It was so painful to watch it all happening without the ability to control any of it. I felt like I wasn't in my body. I was also exhausted and strung out, because remember... I was still using opiates too. But I did not take those pills he stole. Not that it vindicates me in any way. I had to lie through my teeth about my knowledge of it, knowing that they all knew the truth.

So, let's flash back forward. This happy couple had now agreed to let me stay with them. Logically, the hubby let me know very loudly that Jethro was not welcome in his house. I was foolishly defensive because he was in rehab – he was fixing himself, so should be given a chance.

The fact that I was argumentative was so disrespectful. But to be honest, I didn't like this guy... I didn't like him with or without these sad situations. I remember him pulling me aside when their relationship was getting serious. He asked me if he could plan a public announcement and propose to my friend at MY wedding reception. I hardly knew this dude, and still wasn't sure he was any good for my friend... so my thought? No Way. I didn't like the idea.

There were parts of this story where everybody was in the wrong. But that doesn't justify any of the behavior. He went through my stuff, found my socket of weed resin, and assumed it was meth. Then he just waited for the opportunity to use it against me. I'd barely been there for a couple days and my car broke down. Jethro came to fix it and was super offended that he was barred from entry to the house. He fixed my car, left, then my friend's hubby and I got into it. Loudly. He called the cops. He asked them to come get me – said I was on drugs, on meth, psychotic. As I sat in my little room in their house, listening to what he was saying, I felt a pain so deep. My friend never spoke up. She watched it all happen, knowing how badly they had been wronged by Jethro and me. She was trapped between her desire to be a friend to me and her husband's experience of the situation I was in. It sucked.

So, I sat there. I had a couple of pills in front of me. These muscle relaxers. I didn't want to take them. But I wanted to be free of the pain. I put them away – hid them so they wouldn't be found. I felt like I was in hell. So... I pulled out my knife. Jethro insisted that I always carry a knife – because you never know. So I pulled it out, and carved a giant H into my right thigh. Deeply. It hurt. But, it felt better than the pain of listening to what this guy was saying about me in the hall. That wasn't good enough for me. So I carved my calves up too... not as deeply. The pain had subsided. I was comfortably numb. So, just little slices sufficed. I think I took about three or four swipes on each calf. Then the blood started to run and drip on the carpet, so I felt like I should stop. I didn't want to make a mess on my friend's new carpet.

I was now numb. Everything felt better. The cops showed up. I was okay with that. Then the ambulance showed up. I was okay with that too... like I said, I was just numb. I relinquished expectation. I surrendered to whatever would come. At least I wasn't dead. But that was probably what one would call my 'rock bottom'.

This was the last time I spoke regularly with pretty much all my dearest and oldest friends. After that, I was completely alone. I was so full of shame over what happened and felt so much pain for how things had gone. I literally retracted, isolated myself completely and have been without close friends ever since. I speak a little and interact a little with some on social media, but that was back in… God, I don't know, 2008 or 2009. I'm not even sure but I've been pretty much a loner since then.

The lesson? Karmic debt…once again, can be a bitch. I am not sure how or why I earned these lessons, but they were mine to own… and own them I have.

I have peace with it. It taught me deep things about myself. It showed the darkness that I could sink to and stay within, if I so choose. It showed me how dark the world can be when making dark choices.

And truly – I say with a lot of confidence that I am a fucking soldier. Look at what I've been through… what I did. AND… look at me now. Anything is possible.

Chapter 15

That time I had myself a nervous breakdown

I REMEMBER THE END of my marriage to Jethro, I had become so repelled by him. Catching him using needles disgusted me. He even smelled different... I found it repulsive to be around him, let alone sleep with him. Once I got him out of my house, I went to visit him twice. I was still fearful that he would snap, so I wanted to play nice and let him think for a while that I wanted to work things out to help him get used to the idea of being separate. I don't know if it was a good thing or bad thing. The last time I was over there, I had sex with him and it was so unenjoyable. It was literally a pity fuck. I feel so awful admitting that. But... shit... he was still my husband at that point. After that visit, I put up a wall, shutting him out completely.

I was behaving like a goddamn idiot. I had thrown myself into my work. I was there usually six days a week for at least 10 or 11 hours per day. I was in my mid-twenties, a dog Mom who diligently walked my girl so she could handle the away time. I had this boy I was dating (already) who was an old friend from high school and we just hit it off... I'd buy his drinks.... I was enjoying having control over the relationship – being a sugar mama with a powerful job and a cute young man on my arm. He was only a couple of years younger than me, but he was so damn Millennial, and I am a borderline Gen-Xer... it made me feel like a total cougar... which was really fun for me.

This was not a healthy period for me. Outwardly, I lived with all the power of my job, the fun I was having. Inside, I was fearful for my safety, neglecting to take steps to get my divorce finalized from the potentially dangerous man I had just kicked out.

Well the fun I was having was completely idiotic. We used protection at first – only at first, and in my extremely vulnerable state, I found myself falling for this boy hard. Quickly, we were intimate with no form of birth control, but to be honest I wasn't that worried. I had been having unprotected sex with my husband for years and we never got pregnant. I was starting to believe that there was something wrong with my ability to reproduce, and golly... I was just really invested in the destructive behavior in which I was engaged. I told you not all of these stories would be proud moments for me.

Well this boy apparently was from good stock... because before my divorce was even final, I woke up one morning with nausea and figured out pretty quickly that I was pregnant. My first thought was fear for my life. I was scared that Jethro would snap if he found out I had begun an intimate relationship with someone else before our marriage was over. When I went to the boy's house to discuss the situation... he did not have supportive words to offer. The pregnancy was the last thing he wanted. So I was left with not much of a choice. I knew it would cause an enormous mess to have to go through the process of dealing with my court proceedings. If they found out about the pregnancy, it would have required paternity testing to prove that the child was not his and he would then potentially have grounds to use my infidelity against me in the divorce... I had no idea whether or not he would sink that low. I was scared of his intentions, his potential for snapping, and to bring a child into the world without a partner who was ready to be present – I knew I wouldn't have been able to handle things alone in my state.

So... an "A" word was scheduled. I'm not going to go into it. If you've encountered this situation in any way, you know. If you haven't... all I have to say is that it was the absolute worst thing I have ever done. I will never do it again unless it was a medical necessity or requirement to save my own life.

The thought of carrying a child was terrifying in this dumpster fire of a situation. I literally could not handle it. I scheduled as fast as I could – within the first six weeks. I drank heavily during that time. I absolutely hated myself. It was devastating that my first experience with new life had come to fruition in all this madness.

After the abortion, but before the divorce finalized, I went ahead and had myself a little nervous breakdown. I took FMLA leave from my job and attended an outpatient behavioral health program for three weeks. It was on a hospital campus and I would drive there every day.

During this time, I experienced up close my own personal extreme disappointment of our western medical system. They over prescribed meds that I was not comfortable taking and made suggestions to me that were not good solutions. They were giving me a 60mg daily dosage of anti-depressants which I reluctantly agreed to. They tried to prescribe a medicine that would make me not want to drink alcohol. They assumed I was an alcoholic because I confessed how much I was drinking to self-medicate the depression from the abuse and abortion during the divorce. It was definitely the worst part of my dark times – but the thing is... I love normal alcohol consumption. I regulate myself well with it when I am happy. I do have to be mindful when I am struggling. But I am also aware of that. I politely declined that medication.

They tried to prescribe ANOTHER medication when I told them I wasn't sleeping well – medium dosage of Ambien. I angrily declined that. I tried to explain several times that my dead mother had been addicted to pharmaceuticals, that I was healing from an opiate dependency and didn't want a bunch of potentially addictive pharmaceuticals... PLUS, Ambien was a drug Jethro and I had previously abused. My psychiatrist in charge of prescriptions saw me about four times total during my breakdown and a couple of months after – 15 minutes or so a session. Generally, he spent half that time taking calls on his fucking cellphone. One of the times, he apologized lightly saying, *"I'm so sorry, I'm about to go on vacation and there's so much going on."* Oh, please doctor... don't let my horrible life situation get in the way of you nailing down your vacation details. It was disgusting.

They told me to join AA (Alcoholics Anonymous). I tried that with zeal because I had an open mind to any type of healing and figured being around others who were going through a similar hardship might be better than the nurses and doctors who didn't seem to give a flying fuck about me personally.

At the end of my dependency to the opiates, I considered NA (Narcotics Anonymous). I had been to one meeting a few years before to support Jethro. I just felt out of place there. I felt like I was not quite dark enough to even qualify for these meetings... like it was another league of suffering. Not to make light of such a dark time, but I saw myself as Dave Chapelle in *Half Baked* when he tried to go to NA for smoking weed.

I did not find the vibe I was looking for at AA either. It did help to be around others who were overcoming hardship, but I did not feel like I fit in. I found myself sitting around tables with people who spent all their time affirming to themselves and each other that they were broken beyond fixing. I remember the last meeting I attended. There were two people going back and forth about how they were attending these appointments with their psychiatrist and had been put on yet another medication for yet another severe psychological disorder. It was like they lived in this self-perpetuating cycle of finding more and more new things that were wrong instead of focusing on what to do right. The conversation ended with... *"well we just got to hang in there... this is our doing."* I could see their point. But I didn't like where they were being directed. I didn't like that they were buying in to being permanently broken. They were opting to go on extremely strong pharmaceuticals at the recommendation of their doctor without any desire to educate themselves on what that would mean for their life overall... whether the prescriptions were long-term or short-term, what the meds would do to them? This was not the environment for me. I did not feel safe with my own healing there.

I know there are other AA circles out there that are healthier... but my experience left me feeling like my own ability to heal myself would work better than this system. I believe AA is an amazing program for some. Just not me.

My path to deeper healing came in quiet and solitude. I journaled. I meditated. I worked in my garden. I walked my dog. I was able to find solace by doing these types of simple things. When I practiced these rituals regularly, I began to feel like myself again. I felt like I was getting back to who I really was.

However, when I returned to work, everything felt different. My psyche reverted. I felt weak and scared being in the restaurant. Jethro was in the restaurant industry too – and it just felt too close to life as it was with him. I kind of wilted under the weight of the job after my breakdown. I couldn't handle my life as it was before. So I resigned from my high intensity, powerful job.

I ended up finding work in a retail shop where I baked dog treats and it was very good for me at that time. It was gentler work, and I needed that as I recovered from all the darkness and trauma. I didn't keep alcohol in the house for about nine months – to reset my psyche. I drink like a normal person today. I abstain to reset here and there for good measure. It's generally been a safe bet after bad things happen in life because that's when I have a tendency to over consume. I am actually not drinking right now because writing this book has been trigger city. Can't wait for some whiskey in a couple of months.

Jethro did not make things easy for me as I slowly but diligently worked on the divorce. I had to hire a process server to find him because he was dodging the sheriff that was trying to serve the papers to him.

All the while, the boy-toy Toby stuck around. I loved him. Deep down, I was using the relationship as a comforter. A security blanket. When we first dated, he was talking to another woman at the same time. Eight years, two kids and a divorce later... he now lives with her and they are probably going to marry. I feel a degree of guilt for keeping them apart. It seems that they were always meant to be. Karma is such a strange thing.

This period was so dark for me. The breakdown I had helped me get a handle on myself again, but I wasn't the same for years. There was a fragility. Like I had lost a piece of myself. That first marriage and divorce really fractured me. Every once in a while I do get triggered from it for one reason or another and the fragility shows back up... but I always bounce back. I do not wish to have a hat that boasts my victory over this dark time. But, I am extremely proud that I can say I overcame an abusive relationship, a drug dependency, a nervous breakdown and a major depressive episode on my own... in silence.

Chapter 16

When I gave Birth a Couple of Times

WHEN I FIRST BECAME PREGNANT with my son, I read a lot. I was post darkness by more than two years by this time. I was still coming back from my breakdown, still a bit fragile. However... finding out I was pregnant was the most exciting thing for me. I was 28 at the time, and really ready. My initial research was because I was hell bent on making sure I did everything the best I possibly could. One of the best things I read simply stated, "Giving birth is a major life event that you only experience a handful of times or less in your life." I really wanted to make sure I did it right.

I saw a regular OB-GYN initially, but the more times I went for appointments, the less I liked him. I also did some research and found out that he had a high C-section rate – many of which did not have emergency medical reasons. During my pregnancy, I was working at the Healing Arts Center in St. Louis, MO. I am so thankful that I was in such a harmonious environment. Through many lovely conversations with the students and staff in the school, I was lead to do research on having my child in a birth center. The first thing that jumped out at me was that they did not use drugs. I liked this a lot. Most women I know state adamantly that they wanted and happily took 'the drugs' while in labor... epidurals are very common. I figured after everything I've been through, I wanted to do it naturally. I wanted to let myself feel everything, trusting my animal instinct and body to do what it was designed to do. I also figured that I'd be able to handle it.

So there I was, about to have my first child. I was having a boy and I was happy for that. I was not sure I ever wanted to have a girl. I'd never felt like I was any good at understanding them – let alone raising one. Well Divine Design sure saw fit to correct that notion.

My labor and delivery were picture perfect. I handled all of it like a champ. I took really good care of myself during the pregnancy – walked my dogs almost every single day including the day I went into labor. I did prenatal yoga for the last three months. I remember feeling in better physical shape at the end of the pregnancy than the beginning, which made me feel so proud.

I started having contractions in my sleep on a Friday night – woke up to early labor. Since I was under the care of a midwife, I was encouraged to stay comfortable at home and do the things I would usually do until the labor progressed. So... (with some assistance), I walked my dogs, went to the store with Toby and bought a co-sleeper, watched a movie, ate a snack all while having early contractions. It got intense after the sun set – water broke right before we left for the birth center. We arrived there at 8pm and I had him in my arms about 40 minutes later. We were home by 1:30am. Picture. Perfect.

And so was Korben... He was little, weighing in at one ounce less than six pounds. But so was his Dad. Genetics. He gained over two pounds in his first month – he was a great eater and I was a pretty confident milk bank thanks to my own resolve. Nursing went great and I kept him on breast milk until he was 20 months old because he had a slight dairy intolerance.

We found ourselves in Florida as I was weaning him. I was only nursing him a couple of times a day, I was ready to take back my strength. I could feel my energy level shifting as he fed less, so I excitedly began running again. 6am 5k runs – jiggles and all. Once a runner, always a runner. I felt like I was getting myself back.

Then... all the sudden, I got exhausted. Utterly. Exhausted. I was so distressed. I was doing all the right things, feeling good, but I could barely keep myself moving throughout my day. I was falling asleep sitting up at my job. Well... this feeling started to creep up. And the feeling was a suspicion of pregnancy. I just had a feeling.

I was kind of quiet about it, feeling really scared to tell Toby. So... I didn't really speak about my suspicions. Then my period was late. I waited a few days hoping it would come but it never did. I quietly purchased a couple tests. I woke up really early one morning before work because I couldn't sleep and took the test. It was positive.

When he woke up a little while after this, he came out of our tiny little bedroom to the rest of the camper and I was standing there waiting. He asked me,

"What? What's going on?"

"I'm pregnant."

He took a deep breath.

"Okay."

He walked up to me slowly and gave me a timid hug.

I was thankful that he reacted as well as he did. I couldn't take a bad reaction. I didn't have the strength. At this time... I had been making peace with only wanting one child. My first pregnancy was met by him with a kind of detachment. When we decided to have a child together... I cried after the first time we made love because he didn't actually try to impregnate me. Let me repeat that... We DECIDED together that we wanted a child... then he did not try to impregnate me the very first time we made love after that decision was made. So I cried. I suppose we were so bad at communicating that we might have been having completely different conversations in regards to having kids. During the divorce, he brought that up more than once. To be hurtful, he would state that everything was all my fault because I guilted him into having kids with me.

When I found out I was pregnant with Korben, he wasn't particularly celebratory. He loved me, loved my pregnant body, but I never really felt super supported or encouraged. He was already a Dad of two from previous relationships. That probably had something to do with it. I should have taken his behavior as a red flag that he was compromising his own desires to keep me... but also I think part of him did want a family... He was conflicted. I wanted a partner to be excited about pregnancy with me. He wasn't it.

Anyway, I digress... SO... I was pregnant again. Of course, I immediately adjusted my mindset to prepare for bringing another soul into this world. One thing that you cannot get away from as a female: If you are charged with bringing a soul into this world, it becomes the absolute most important job you do. The end. More important than your work, your opinion, your feelings about the pregnancy. That soul is yours to grow and bring from the ethers into this world. I hold that with the utmost importance after what I've been through.

I was convinced that we were having another boy. The pregnancies just felt the same. When we had our sex reveal ultrasound and she said 'girl', we looked at each other with confused and slightly fearful faces. I understand boys. I am comfortable with males. My understanding of women was non-present with the lack of Mom and friends and all. I was pretty nervous to have a girl. But I must say... Astrid is the best blessing I could have ever imagined. She is so strong and passionate. She is so sassy, and she teaches me how to be a stronger woman. Already. She's three. I am truly thankful for my daughter.

My pregnancy was splendid. I am extremely good at being pregnant. In fact, while pregnant with my second, my mind was really changed about how many children I wanted. I felt so positive, so blessed to grow my children with comfort, confidence and a sound mind. It started to feel to me like it was part of my blessed calling to bring souls into the world. I got a tiny touch of hypertension in the pregnancy, carried lower and had some pain near the end... but I was working full-time this time around and also chasing around a toddler. I felt like I handled it like a champ. Similarly to Korben, it was a perfect pregnancy to me.

As we got closer to the big day, we prepared. All this time, Toby had mostly stayed home with Korben and looked after the house. We did get an apartment about halfway through the pregnancy, because our tiny 200 square-foot camper was not going to be comfortable for a nine-months-pregnant lady. We found this crappy apartment that was even closer to the intercostal, which was fine by me. There was a park walking distance away with a lake and pathway.

The week before going into labor, I asked Toby to be prepared in a couple of basic ways. First, he needed to be ready to send Korben to the on-call helper. Next, I needed him to know the way to the birth center so he could drive us there without having to ask me stupid questions while I'm breathing through contractions. We had a bunch of different due dates over the span of a nine day period – because of when my period landed and ultrasound results... so we had no idea when she would actually come. I remember showing up to work on that last Friday. Pregnant as fuck. My temporary replacement whom I had recruited and trained was this lovely young woman... she was there already taking care of things. My boss came around the corner and asked what on Earth I was doing there. She gave me a quick acupuncture treatment and sent me home. She told me I'd be having a baby this weekend. It didn't feel like it to me... She felt like she was still hanging tough in there, and we still had two other tentative due dates coming up in the next week.

So... I went home and we took Korben to the beach. We walked. We held his hands and played. It was a beautiful day. A couple of ladies shouted out,

"You look great, when are you due?"

I said,

"Any day!"

They answered with laughter,

"Keep going girl!"

Well, apparently, I was in early labor for who knows how long. I got home from the beach tired, had a normal rest of the evening with Korben, then showered and got ready for bed. Right as I began to dose off... my eyes shot open because my water broke. It felt like I was peeing my pants, but it was coming from somewhere else. It just flowed out. So, my immediate reaction was panic. It was almost 11pm. My ex mother-in-law had just flown out of town and our on-call was my ex father-in-law who was now by himself and probably in bed. And it was fucking 11pm.

The plan began. The midwife on call told me to hang tight. She was with another Mom who was giving birth at home. She told me to put on a pad and tell me how full it got in an hour and call her back. The pad was soaked through in minutes.

So, I was in labor. And my midwife/nurses on call were spread thin. I stayed at home as long as I could, packed a suitcase, but forgot food. I just wasn't ready for it to happen so quickly. We left the house around 1am. The contractions were very intense, and it felt like the labor would go a lot quicker with this one.

Here's where Toby threw another loud red flag. He never made the simple effort to google the birth center and figure out for himself where he would be driving me. The directions were easy as fuck and yet... I had to scream when to turn right and left through the contractions and the curse words. It was great. I was not happy about that.

When we arrived, no one was there yet because they had not one but two other Moms giving birth at their homes at the same time. A few minutes after our arrival, their office manager/nurse assistant arrived and got us all set up. She got the bath water running in our suite and I immediately jumped in (figuratively), feeling much better.

Astrid was ready to come when she was ready to come. I think she came out so quickly because her umbilical cord got wrapped a couple of times so it sent her into a panic. The nurse was able to quickly reverse one wrap, and relieve the other. So that was that... She was in my arms before 3am. All in all I was in active labor for less than four hours. I was home by 6:30am, Korben came home around 11am after a nap had been taken with the brand-new baby.

My children were born into warm water in dimly lit rooms and gentle hands that caught them. They were placed immediately onto my bare body. When I was moved from the tub to the bed, they spent some skin-to-skin time with their Dad.

I birthed them in two different states, over a thousand miles apart. My experiences bringing them to this Earth are two of the most beautiful, important memories I have ever made. They say that after childbirth, a chemical is released to help the woman forget the intensity of labor so she will not be afraid to birth children again. I tell you with all my heart that I actively recall those nights and remember them vividly to my delight. I truly loved the experiences.

I also love that someday, the one I love might want a kid. We will have a discussion where I will be able to share my birth experiences and express confidence in my ability to do it again with just as much success. He and I will be able to decide together if that's what we want. I love that the option is there.

If I'm being super honest, I feel that being queer allowed me to carry my pregnancies better. I am proud of how it went. It was such a great contrast to all the dark things that happened in years previous. It made me feel truly healed. Like I had truly conquered anything life could ever throw at me. Little did I know that I'd have to endure one more messy divorce before I finally closed the book on my suffering.

Chapter 17

That Time I Lived like a Missionary in a Third world country on American soil

IN 2015, TOBY AND I had a weird series of events occur that led us to do something super crazy. Looking back now, it probably wasn't the wisest decision... although I will say that our travels helped me recognize a pattern he repeated that would have left me unhappy for years had I not figured it out. But... that's not the focus. For the most part, these travels were absolutely amazing and very educational.

A little back story: We were living in a little rental house in St. Charles, Missouri. Both of us had full-time jobs, and Korben was about 13 months old. I got my taxes done, and it was amazing to see how much money an unwed mother who works part time gets back from the government. It was a significant nest egg. When we found out how much we were getting, of course the questions became... what should we do with this money?

The first logical answer was buy a house. So we started looking. We started fantasizing about what kind of house we wanted, what neighborhood... It was really fun! Then... Korben got sick. The health department got called in to his daycare because of an outbreak of a viral stomach infection. I was hopeful that it wouldn't get him, but about a week into the outbreak, I got the call that he had diarrhea and had to be picked up.

I left work and headed straight there. The poor boy was so dehydrated for the next week or so. The complicated nature of the health department being involved was what caused a serious ruffle in our family feathers. He was barred from returning to daycare until the health department received the following from us: 1. A stool sample to prove he did indeed have the sickness that was going around the daycare. 2. A doctor's note stating that he had been given antibiotics. 3. He had to run through the antibiotics for at least seven days. 4. His stool had to be retested and get a negative result for him to be released and be brought back to school.

Overall, the ridiculousness of this kept him out of school and me out of work for over three weeks. It sucked up all my sick time, all my vacation time, every personal day, and eventually I was just out of work without pay. One of the days, I had to be at work and Toby called in to bring Korben to the doctor. He got written up at work for calling in last minute.

We were both outraged, annoyed, frustrated. We looked around at our life. My son was still nursing and I missed being home with him (I had just gone back to work full-time a few months earlier). We were both on thin ice at work because of the daycare situation.

We both felt like the situation was a metaphor for the rat race of life, and were just so sick of being around people. We got cold feet about buying a house. We looked around at our lives and felt trapped by what we were doing. We didn't want to be stuck in the same place for 30 years in some house somewhere. It sounded awful.

During this same period, I was undergoing an extreme metaphysical shift... My gifts started showing up and there was so much revelation and confusion about my life on Earth. I was so done with the status quo answers to how to live life according to the 'typical' rules. I wanted something that spoke to my spirituality – that spoke to my soul.

So... we happened to have this buddy who was working at a National Forest that was a concessionary camp ground. Every year, they needed people out there to work as camp hosts... clean the bathrooms, mow the lawns, take money from the campers, keep an eye on the grounds... The guy who managed the concession lived there part of the year and lived in Arizona the rest of the year. He was a successful entrepreneur and our buddy had been there for a couple of years.

He described the life he had in such a way – we were so intrigued. It was a life that anyone would dream of. Working for yourself, a quiet life, in the forest, no cities for miles... We thought for a while about this. How would it work with a child? How would we make ends meet? How the fuck would we get there? Where would we live? After a lot of thought and some conversations with our friend, we decided that we were being called out there.

This was a serious move for us. It would require selling/trading both of our cars in for a tow vehicle, selling most of our possessions, moving our whole lives into an amount of stuff that we could transport in an SUV – including two cats and two dogs.

We had a garage sale, donated so much stuff, listed furniture on Craigslist. We sold one of the cars on

Craigslist also. The other we traded for a Durango – after doing a lot of research on what would be affordable, but also practical for pulling a rig. Then we started researching campers. What kind to get, how to take care of them, how to hitch them, how to flush and clean the tanks... There was so much to learn, but we were studying our asses off. We did research on people who live in their campers year round. We learned about how it's possible to stay mobile and make a living, but be completely free of the usual crap that is typical when you are a regular society dweller.

We learned from salesmen on the phone when shopping for hitches that this was a movement gaining momentum in this country. There are lots of people that were going 'off-grid' and living a more transient life.

It all sounded so amazing. We felt full of confidence that this was the life for us. I was going to write, work on my spiritual practice and look after Korben while Toby would do the camp host work. We were promised that we would make a great little nest egg by the end of the season, and that there was potential for us to stay on later and work as 'trimmigrants' in the fall. This is the nickname given to the people who showed up to trim buds for the blooming marijuana industry in Oregon. Did I mention this was in Oregon? At the time, weed was medically and recreationally legal there – and only a handful of other states in the country.

So we were slowly seeing all the pieces of the potential plan come together. We planned financially to have enough money to stay afloat through the season – and thought up back-up plans to the back-up plans.

Well none of it went as well as we hoped – except for the parts where we were travelling. We passed through fifteen states in all – my favorite parts were Wyoming and Nevada. So beautiful out there. There are such fewer people – it's so much quieter and divine.

When we got to the camp hosting job – we discovered that we were right back where we started (figuratively). We had to work with a guy (not our friend) who was the epitome of someone you HATE to work with. Just not a nice person. So... we spent all that money, time, sacrifice of comfort to end up with the same basic complaints of working in a lame office somewhere. It was quite a karmic lesson.

Meanwhile, my dog tore her ACL chasing ground squirrels, chipped a tooth, and broke her tail. It was so wild, it was too wild. I had a moment of fear at the vet because it occurred to me that eventually something equally worrisome might happen to our little human. AND... the closest human hospital was 40 minutes away. It got me scared.

We took a week thinking about what to do... and decided that we should move on before we ran out of money. We spent a ridiculous amount of money on vet bills and the way we were going to get paid at the campgrounds just wasn't going to cut it. The guy in charge made promises that panned out differently in real life – he ended up screwing over our friend in the end as well.

After some conversation... we decided Florida would be fun. We had family there, Toby had gone to school there... he spoke often about how he loved going to school there. But that in the end of his schooling, it had become very lonely. He wanted to share the beauty of Florida with me. It sounded lovely.

In all reality, this trip was just another example of Toby's restless spirit. He became angry with situations so quickly – even when we should have been feeling like we were in paradise everywhere we roamed. I enjoyed our travels so much, but there were points that we fought so badly I didn't think we would make. Obviously I was right.

Chapter 18

The Florida Times

THE LEG OF THE TRIP FROM northwest to southeast was driven mostly by me. Toby got nervous really easily towing the 28-foot rig on the highway – when the wind blew it was quite powerful. He was better at doing the fine maneuvering.... Backing her into spots on lots. I was the one who was good at highway driving. So here we were, driving down to Florida. We barely had enough money to get ourselves started there (with help from his parents), but we had a destination to park at least for the first few nights, so it was alright.

We made the drive as quickly as we could. It was a beautiful drive. Korben was such a good little traveler too, which was amazing in my eyes. We arrived in Florida pretty late one evening, and parked the rig in his parents' driveway. They had just sold their house and were getting ready to move. We were going to hang there with them for a week or two until we could settle in somewhere.

His parents insisted that we relax for a while... take a breather from all the stress of travelling. So we spent a couple days at the beach, going out for dinners with them. But I could not relax. There was, of course, an immediate urgency to figure out how I was going to take care of my family. We couldn't stay parked in this driveway and somebody needed a job. So I was hunting for where we could go and what I could do. Within about two weeks, I found a great RV park to call home AND was offered a job. I was going to be managing an acupuncture office – with four D.O.M's (acupuncturists) and an LMT (massage therapist) upstairs. In Florida, acupuncturists are able to bill insurance. D.O.M. stands for Doctor of Oriental Medicine. It was great pay, and the environment was my cup of tea.

The RV park charged reasonable rent, was close to the intercostal and was dog-friendly. Depending on where you are from – you may or may not by cringing at the idea of a young family living in an RV park. In places like Florida, Oregon, Colorado, New Mexico, California... RV people are considered normal people. It's actually a great way of living... of being. There were families just like us that lived in these parks – by choice. It keeps you outside more, teaches you about only keeping possessions that are important. It's impossible to become a hoarder when you don't have enough space to accumulate stuff.

We were settling in. It was lovely. We were looking forward to a summer of fun. His parents were excited to babysit here and there – so we weren't completely without support. We could go rent jet-skis, paddle boards, play in the ocean, and save up money for the next leg of the journey we were on.

Fourth of July weekend, I had been working at Art of Acupuncture in St. Petersburg for a couple of weeks. I was feeling strong.

This was when I found out I was pregnant again.

Toby did alright during the pregnancy, but became increasingly angry with life. Again. When Christmas time came around, I got really excited because he always spoke about this awesome Christmas festival in Dunedin which was near where we lived. I desperately wanted him to take me there. I wanted him to show me his fondness for Florida when he spoke about it during our travels. I told him this. He never took me to the festival.

Also, I spent Christmas alone that year. He and Korben traveled up to St. Louis with his parents so they could celebrate with their family and see his daughter. Korben also got to spend time with my family which was good. I was seven months pregnant and not feeling up to the car travel. So Christmas Day in 2015, I went to the beach alone, listened to Dark Side of the Moon, sunbathed, soaked in the ocean and took this really gorgeous photo of a cloud that looked like a dragon eating the sun. I also spent a lot of time gaming while they were gone. If you must know, I was playing *The Elder Scrolls: Skyrim* and it was glorious. I purchased it for Toby for Christmas, but it was for this bitch, too. It was really relaxing. It was also really lonely.

Then Toby, once again, became outright miserable. The obsession became about how much he hated Florida... hated the people, hated the drivers, hated everything there was to hate. He and his Dad started looking for land to purchase back in Missouri. He was convinced that if we moved back to the forest and lived off the land again, things would be fine. This time, I had outgrown jumping on the misery bandwagon with him. But, I was very pregnant and post-partum during this period. I did not have the strength to argue anymore. If it had been up to me, I would have stayed in Florida. I liked it there. I liked my job, I liked the friends I was making. I liked being next to the ocean.

This run in Florida showed me one last important thing before we left... It was May. I had gotten a job with the YMCA at the ranch and we were packed up, ready to move to the newly purchased acreage and develop it.

Astrid had been to the beach one time, but I did not dip her little feet into the ocean because Toby was in too bad of a mood... again. So... before we were ready to drive away... I asked,

> *"Can we please go drive over the intercostal one more time to say goodbye to the ocean, and dip Astrid's little feet in so she can say she's touched the ocean?"*

> *"Fuck the ocean."*

Was the response.

> *"I'm fucking done with this place, fuck going there."*

That, my friends... was the moment that I knew my second marriage was doomed. It was May of 2016. I spent the next couple of years trying my hardest to make it work... to accept it and keep my family together... but truly... This moment solidified in my mind that this person was not who I wanted to spend my life with. I uprooted everything for him, traveled thousands of miles with him, bore children with him... and no matter what we did he just showed up miserable everywhere we went. He wasn't for me and I clearly wasn't for him. I hung on for way too long afterward in due diligence, but at least I can say I tried. I truly did.

Chapter 19

My Weight Loss Journey

WE ALL KNOW WHAT IT IS to fluctuate with our weight. I actually became underweight several times in early adulthood – I was a stress faster. At 16 years old I weighed about 100 pounds during a stressful time. I'm 5'6" and that put me at 20 pounds underweight. I've also been on the other side – my heaviest weight was carrying my second child at 213 pounds. Post-partum I landed around 180.

That being said, I think it's important to acknowledge that it is equally difficult to lose OR gain weight. Anyone on a journey that is accomplishing either of these things... I commend you.

When I became pregnant with my first child, I was chubby and deconditioned. I did not work out, I lived a sedentary life. The only physical activity was walking my dogs and I did not do that regularly.

Fast forward to the end of that pregnancy... I barely gained 25 pounds because I actually lost weight in the first trimester. I decided I wanted to do things right so I walked every day and changed my diet. I was actually taking longer, brisker walks at the end of the pregnancy than the beginning.

Before the second pregnancy I had gotten back down to a size eight in blue jeans... WHAT, WHAT! Sadly, I gained more weight because I was working full-time and was much more exhausted. Plus I love food. I ate my feelings a lot.

I Broke 200 pounds – and stayed up there for about the last trimester. That bummed me out. Directly postpartum I lost about 15 pounds. As I mentioned previously, I trickled down to about 180 and stayed around there until I was ready to really work on my body (after nursing).

So... 16 months later.... Still at the same weight, daughter almost completely weaned... I decided to start running again. I knew training would be easy for me. So the road to reclaiming my body began.

I ran or did the elliptical about three times a week. That helped because jogging with all the jiggles from nursing boobies and rolls acquired whilst making babies really made it hard for me to want to run. I was feeling self-conscious this time around.

Slowly, my endurance returned. I was feeling stronger and it was lovely! However, I was not really losing any of the weight I wanted to lose. So for motivation, I decided to up the game. I signed up for an OCR... an Obstacle Course Race. These things are amazing! They can be dangerous: the ones that are more for fun have volumes of people that don't always take it seriously so you really have to step carefully. The serious ones are just plain challenging. However, I felt up to the challenge.

The first one I did was meant as a gesture to my Brother. He had started running OCR's and I wanted to find a new way to bond with him in adulthood. We grew apart for some of our middle years. As we've grown back together, it's been nice feeling like I could find new ways to be friends with him again. The first one was great – it was a 5k with about 15 obstacles. My Brother chose the Warrior Dash because the proceeds went to St. Jude's (cancer research). Since he's a fucking marine, he finished near the front of his heat. I finished the race – not impressively, but I sure as shit completed every obstacle.

That got me hungry for more, so I started shopping for a next race... a tougher race.

The next course I chose was called Green Beret. Why this one? At the time, I had a mentor and coach at work who encouraged me to do it. And I was up for the challenge. A 5-mile, 25 obstacle course that focused on 'carries.' This meant carry a sandbag for a quarter mile, a ruck sack, two handle sandbags, and at the very end... a yolk carry through a creek of waist high water and boulders/branches scattered throughout. There were also rope challenges. It. Was. Insanity. There were a couple obstacles on this one I could not complete because of my body weight. In my training, I did a shit ton of running and calisthenics. I did not lift weights, and I really should have. My arms and hands were not strong enough to carry me up a rope. So... that kept me from being able to complete a couple of the challenges.

I was so proud of myself for completing this race. At the time, I was still pretty chunky. I looked around at all the other competitors and they were ripped... sporting serious scowls on their faces... like we were all enemies. I guess if you were competing for a qualifying spot in the OCR Nationals, then yes, I get the scowls. But for me, I was smiling. I was looking around like a complete nerd for a friendly face... I wanted to smile and wave at everybody and give a bunch of thumbs-ups. I was just happy to be there and feel confident enough to actually go through with the race.

At that point, I was still about 173 pounds. Had not lost much weight. That was in June of 2018. At the time, I was separated from Toby. We were still living in the same house, not sure what we were going to do.

After the race, I felt so happy and accomplished. Since things were strained between us, he did not come to support me. I approached him that weekend to have some conversation. I tearfully asked him what he wanted, what were we going to do? He bluntly, quietly told me that he thought I should move back home to St. Louis.

So, in a flurry of pain and desperation… I began job hunting. Interestingly enough, I did not have much trouble finding something that sounded absolutely perfect! It was a management position for a kickboxing studio that would be opening in the St. Louis area. At that time, I was so fitness focused. I had a very respectable position as a resort director and lots of management experience, so it seemed like a logical choice. When I submitted the application, I received a phone call from the owner less than 30 minutes later.

Long story short, I was offered the job and put in my notice at The Y. This was the start of quite a stressful time in my life.

Enter into my life stage right: Ilovekickboxing.com. A franchise run by some of the most amazing people I have ever encountered. I worked for a St. Louis based studio for about six months and I've remained a member taking the classes for almost a year now.

This opportunity was no fucking joke. The classes are absolutely badass. I felt like I was in decent shape after my race, because it was not easy. After taking some downtime to nurse a calf injury, I went for my first ILKB class in July of 2018. Once again – no fucking joke. I got through it and made an immediate determination that I had a long way to go in regards to my physical fitness. A challenge that was very exciting for me.

As an athlete, I remember waking up one and two days after my first workout, looking forward to the analysis of how sore I would feel, where I would feel it most. I tell you... I stepped out of bed, walked to the kitchen, and noticed the most perfect... equally distributed, moderate, all over body soreness as I moved around that morning. My inner athlete was hashtag impressed. Nothing was outrageously tough to do, but clearly the workout was going to sculpt literally EVERYTHING on my body. I was hooked. It has been quite some time since I had pursued any sort of organized, guided fitness routine. I was really looking forward to feeling like a real athlete again.

I began training two to three times a week in early August. I also still went on road runs, but at the time my calf was still giving me trouble when I ran. The kickboxing did not seem to be affected by it, which was a blessing.

In late August, I attended a bootcamp at the ILKB headquarters in Long Island, New York. The physical portion of the training was amazing. I felt like an idiot being on the mat with other people who were in so much better shape, but I knew what I was made of underneath my Mom bod. At this point... I was still weighing in right around 170 pounds... all sorts of fat, not much muscle. I literally had a trucker gut.

At first, I barely had the ability to balance myself when throwing a roundhouse. I would literally have to brace myself on the bag after a kick to stay on my feet. The coaches at the boot camp were so helpful. Coaching is something I've always been very responsive to as an athlete. It's just a style that gets through to me. I had this school girl admiration for this one in particular. I remember feeling so much appreciation every time he stopped by to give me guidance as I worked on my technique in class. He remained the person I admired the most from the headquarters during my time with the company.

With such helpful guidance, I was feeling pretty strong within a couple of months. The weight loss started coming – quickly. For a single month, I did jump into a supplement regimen to help with the weight loss. It kick started everything, but I did not stick with it because it just wasn't in my budget.

It was also a very stressful time for me. I had to move residences four fucking times total as I transitioned into the single person/single parent life. It had a negative effect on my performance at life on a pretty consistent basis. But I always had my training. I took class a lot during this time. It kept me steady more than I realized.

Once November hit, I had this all of the sudden realization that it was becoming blue jeans weather. I was shocked and overjoyed to discover that EVERY SINGLE pair of jeans from the previous winter were way too big on me when I pulled out the cold weather gear.

So I went shopping! I have no idea how or when it happened, but in the course of this six month period of all this transition for me... I went from wearing a 12-14 to a size 4 in jeans. Seriously.

No matter what, the training continued consistently. All the fat slowly disappeared, but then I had all this change to my body that was initially really depressing. My breasts were completely different, and my ass looked deflated.

Well, I kept with it and realized that slowly all that extra space where the fat had once been was steadily and surely being replaced with new, dense, and beautiful muscle mass. My arms are a point of pride for me now. They are not without fat. There is still most definitely squish everywhere, but there are also really beautiful, defined muscles.

So... in January of 2019 I finally stopped worrying over losing anymore. I'm down to a weight I haven't seen on the scale since high school and college, and I am still gaining more muscle. Overall, I lost about 40 pounds. I have maintained my current shape for about six months now.

I don't do fancy diets. I drink whiskey and wine and beer. I portion control, drink enough water, and train regularly! I always try to make two to three classes a week. It doesn't always happen with my work schedule and time with the kids, but I do my very best. I've joined a second gym and I now lift weights and I'm running again. I want to build more muscle, because people – I think if we really keep this all up, we are going to age SO well. That's what I want. My intention is to still be a runner, lifter and kickboxer all the way until the day I die. It keeps me steady and sane.

As I've mentioned before, I've been an athlete my whole life. From my heart, the years I spent growing and nursing children really took a toll on my overall strength... on a soul level. I stayed active... but my body was exhausted from it. I became pregnant in March of 2013. I nursed my son for 20 months until I was two months pregnant with my daughter. I nursed my daughter for 16 months. SO... a combined time giving milk from my body of three years... with no break in between. During this time, as I discovered my identity and wanted to own it... I felt a lot of conflict and lack of support. It was isolating and emotionally exhausting. Regaining my confidence through physical fitness was so much more important that just fitting into smaller clothes. Especially when I became a single parent.

It remains really scary going out in public with young kids... running scenarios where I might have to get them to the car if one of them has a meltdown in public. All. By. Myself. I have physical anxiety at that thought. My strength from this journey allows me to carry them both at the same time if I absolutely have to. It allows me to carry one of them for a pretty long time when I need to. It allows me to run and play with them as if I were a kid because I am in good enough shape. My physical fitness has become so much more than my own in these crucial years where they are still so dependent on me.

ASIDE from that – it was extremely awesome to watch my physique do its thang. As I became more and more sculpted, my androgyny became more beautiful to me. My masculinity became more obvious. Now, more than ever, I hear people say I look so much like my Dad – something I haven't heard since I was a young pre-pubescent child. It's been weird getting used to myself in the mirror as a queer – but this helped me feel attractive in a new way. It's like all that desire I had to be able to do anything a guy could do was finally reflected on the outside as I felt on the inside. I thank the Powers that Be for this journey.

Currently, I am working on revisions for this book, in the middle of a month-long period with a lot of travel for work and I have not taken class in two weeks. I. Am. Dying. I don't see a therapist, I don't take pharmaceuticals... I manage myself with meditation, physical fitness and self-care. BUT the physical fitness stuff is so crucial. It's two fold. It is one of the best ways to generate and maintain prana while helping with my chemical imbalance naturally. Old pain knows just how to sneak up on me when I am not able to work out.

It's crucial for my mental health. Also, I have new friends who really care about me. They miss me when I am not in class. We sweaty hug each other and encourage each other. It has completed a circle for me that was broken when I was in a lonely place in my life. Remember that time when I lost all of my friends? I finally have new ones.

So... that's my weight lost journey. It's way more than just a weight loss journey. It's also a wellness journey. It is not over. It continues every day. I give love to my body and mind this way. I don't really look at the scale much. I look at how my clothes fit, and I note how I feel about myself. I most certainly still have jiggles and squishy spots all over my body. But I love those. They are part of my individuality.

Chapter 20

Surviving

LET'S RECAP... I am not going to make a list of everything tough I've been through... it would not be productive. But... I do like to acknowledge that I came through it. Having said that... I'd like to dedicate some pages to talk about what it is to be in survival mode. It's a place I have occupied off and on for a significant amount of time. I lived in survival mode as a child when Mom was having tough spells. I lived in survival mode for years following her death. I stayed there in survival mode until I was well into high school.

The survival mode switched on and off during my two failed marriages – depending on the situation... I should have been much more concerned than I was at many points, but feeling in love with someone was completing.

It felt right when it felt right, even if it was a sub-par form of love.

The second divorce was less messy in many ways, but worse in others because there were children involved... children who had an awareness of what was going on.

I want to be honest about something. After all the separations and trouble we had over the last couple years in our run, it was a conversation with my son that finally pushed me over the line into deciding to leave him for good.

We were having a fight – another bad fight. This was late September. Toby would always storm outside after intense moments so he could angrily smoke a cigarette. I sat on the couch, my head bowed into my hands... with angry tears and a heavy heart. Both kids were in the room. The younger was detached to the fighting still at this point, but Korben was pretty tuned in. He approached me and we had the following conversation...

"Mama."

"Yes, baby."

"Mama," as he placed his hands on my legs and looked me in the eye,

> "How 'bout this... how 'bout when we move, you and me and Astrid can go to the new house together, and Dada could stay in this house and we could just find a new Dada? How about that?"

"Oh, baby."

I didn't even know how to answer. I think I apologized to him and gave him a big hug... said something like it was all going to be alright.

In my head, I was screaming and weeping. I saw my future. I saw years of watching my children observe me compromising my own happiness in order to keep our family together. I saw them witnessing fights, separations, I saw that I would be teaching them to forfeit happiness if I stayed with this guy.

I saw their little faces observe how much we weren't working together. At this time, Korben was four years old. Fucking four years old. He had this notion in his head without any prompting from me. His beautiful, innocent, free flowing logic and wisdom inspired him to suggest this to me as a solution for the pain we were all feeling. Not for any one individual, but because I think he sensed it would make for a happier ending for everyone.

So... that conversation gave me the push to finally close my heart on Toby. And I did. I flipped a switch, and stopped trying to love our potential. I had been falling out of love with him since the Florida times, but I really tried hard to make things work and that got me two and a half more years deep into this wrong relationship. I don't regret it... I feel satisfied that I truly tried.

I used him to help me move into the new house. He even came with me, but I was done with him. We were hardly sleeping together at that point. Mostly, it was out of primal desire for me and I had to be drunk to really want to. Before then, it had become about a once-a-month thing. I just lost attraction to him as a person.

I had one slip-up in late November... I traveled to New York for a bootcamp once more and was feeling heartbroken and confused. After the work stuff was over, I took some time to explore the city and just try and enjoy life for a second. I went and visited a psychic – a mistake on my part. I watched her pull cards from her deck and noticed that it was stacked with the major arcana heavy hitters that a confused and heartbroken person would want to see. But... she got some main points correct right at the beginning, so in my vulnerable state, I was hooked.

During this time – something strange was happening to me. I was experiencing this strange pull towards someone. It was mystical – a really strong curiosity that I cannot completely describe. It was an attraction that was incredibly overwhelming, but it was very confusing for me. He lived very far away and we hardly knew one another... I had this sense that he was calling out to me – expressing this secret interest in me. But, I hadn't dated or flirted with another person in eight years, so I was left feeling like a confused tourist in a foreign country. I had expressed an interest out loud in seeing him right around that time and received a cold shoulder from him... so the confusion and hurt was screaming from two different directions... Toby and this other mysterious heart connection that I could not shake no matter how hard I tried.

Well in this moment with the psychic, I had no one. Both of these men, for different reasons, were detached from me. Toby had started seeing the woman who is now his super nice and awesome future wife. The mystery man just stayed a mystery, extending a polite thanks but no thanks and then simple silence when I made attempts to explore this strange attraction I felt.

Once more... I was confused as fuck. So the psychic – was a poor idea. She read for me and said that I needed to make up with 'this man'. That I was destined to have one more child and it was with 'this man' because he was truly my soul mate. Which fucking man?! I doubted in my heart that this new love interest could possibly be considered part of the picture. The only other choice was going back to Toby.

So I did... to my shame. When I got home, I told him I wanted to try and see if things could mend. That I wanted to have another kid. We went out to dinner to talk. I slept with him again. He agreed to having another child even though in previous conversations he expressed that he was very much done having kids. But he was desperate too. He loved the idea of me. He loved that he had possession of me. But he didn't really love being married to me. He didn't really like who I was. If he did, he would have treated me differently for the years that we spent together.

After falling back in towards him... I felt sure. Absolutely fucking sure that it was over. Why? Because after going out for a meal to talk about things, going to bed with him... watching him feel so happy and relieved to be putting up Christmas décor together as a family... all I felt was... anxiety. It didn't feel right. In fact, it felt really, really wrong. Like it physically hurt to be doing what I was doing with him.

I told him so. He cried and then became so angry. He said all sorts of things speaking to my horrible decisions and who I was as a person for doing this to him 'again'. It was awful. I felt just horrible. But at least I was sure about what really, really needed to happen.

Truly, I gave it every effort to make it work.

So, the next steps were difficult as fuck and did cost me my well-paying job managing that oh-so-fantastic kickboxing studio. It was a sales driven position. When things with the separation and divorce were going okay.... sales were great. When we had difficult weeks – like that one time he took the kids from me for a week saying I was an unfit mother – the sales and my ability to perform my job absolutely tanked.

This was January. In December, I publicly launched my own start-up – my healing practice online. I wanted to transition to it slowly. I wanted to be doing the subtle, ethereal work that I was best at full-time, but I was still trying to figure out how it would actually play out. I was also healing myself, and didn't want to jump into it full throttle just yet.

The owner of the studio I managed observed the expression of my true desires… he saw me launching my site and my public presence. He heard the groanings of the staff at the studio when I was showing up emotionally compromised and he eventually had enough.

As we were interviewing for the assistant manager, I was completely checked out of the job anyway. I was so unhappy. Not with the job – with me. I felt like I was failing at everything. And it poured out everywhere. I also did not get along the best with the owner. He and I did not always see eye to eye. I really wanted to leave the company, but I felt trapped by obligation to make a living for the kids.

At the conclusion of the week, the owner sat me down and basically let me know he was managing me out. He gave me a month notice and offered to let me stay on hourly. I admit this was very gracious. Nevertheless, I did not want that at all. The things he communicated that the staff had said about me left me feeling completely uninterested in keeping a relationship as an employee. I think what hurt the most was that none of them were willing to come to me with their concerns. These young women were all gifted and talented. In months previous I very specifically asked them to pull me aside and have a conversation if they ever had concerns or disagreed with how things were going from my end. That literally never happened. They all went to him instead. I've been told I come off as very scary sometimes... or maybe they just felt bad because of my personal situation. I don't know. My role there now is nothing more than a business to business member. I offer their members discounts for my services. I am still proud to represent the studio and be an advocate for the brand... they do amazing work for the members and it's still a happy place for me.

I am more than okay with it. Turns out, it was the best thing that could have ever happened to me. It created a discomfort that motivated me to really examine what I wanted out of life.

Circling back around, the 'survival mode' was once more in full throttle. I suppose I found comfort in this mode. It was a sort of a way of life for me. But that is not how life is supposed to be.

So now – I sit here typing. I am in a hotel room working an amazing program where I am teaching self-care, meditation, and new age wisdom to the most amazing, receptive and kind older adults you could ever imagine as part of a wellness program I designed.

This morning, I relaxed. This work – teaching, healing, writing... it feels more right than anything else I have ever done in my entire life.

What I have been through is taking me to heights I could have never imagined. My practice... my business... This is my future. It's going to bring a new knowing to you. You – the reader – for whom my heart bleeds.

Because after everything that has happened to me... the most important work that I hold in my heart... is you. I want to help every single human being on this Earth learn that they are just as magickal, gifted, strong and capable as anybody's favorite historical avatar. There are no ifs, ands, or buts about it.

Everything is possible. Anything is possible. Even when one is in survival mode.

So... a shit ton of trauma and drama later... Not really any worse for the wear. I might not know what the future holds for me exactly, but survival mode is over. I've realized that living in the flow of universal synchronicity completely defeats the need for it. It creates within me a knowing... that everything is truly happening exactly as it is meant to.

Thank you, thank you... anything bad that ever happened. I have purged the imprint and respect the memory. I have found my way to my Beloved Family. My children are cared for. My heart is open to love. My little birdie tells me be patient... and trust.

Chapter 21

When my Gifts Showed Up

WE READ AND HEAR STORIES all the time of gifted individuals... psychics, mediums, empaths, etc. These are the amazing beings that are holding the frontlines of the Aquarian banner of change. Many of them have been seeing things, hearing things, knowing things since they were young children. I am not one of these. My gifts were hidden away from me for quite a long time. Why? Trauma. I would not have been able to handle what was happening. Moreover, I did not have a mentor capable of helping me sort through what was going on. So... they laid dormant until the time was right.

Turns out the time was right when I was thinking about and approaching motherhood. I cannot honestly tell you if the event I'm about to describe happened before or after the birth of my first child – I think it was after. I think the flood of hormones mixed with my recognition of how absolutely divine and magickal I was in relation to this tiny human finally convinced the Powers that Be I was ready.

Here is how it happened for me.

I started channeling things... Things I did not understand. It was people – sometimes their voices. More than anything else, it was their bodies. I would dance and move into this trance state where my movements were not my own. I was me, but I was also being occupied by something else. Sometimes I had a vague awareness of what that something might be. Other times... it was a complete mystery.

One of the people is someone that I still commune with regularly. I have a partner in energy. If we are getting technical – he is my descendent from a past life. Boom. Wrap your head around that business... I'll be diving into the specifics of this amazing connection in my next book – I suggest you stay tuned because it is interesting. He is a Medicine Man in South America. I do not know his name. He does not know mine. But we have a connection that is beyond space and time. We draw power from one another, divining information, healing, diplomacy and comfort. Why did we connect? Because our souls are family.

He was the first specific instance that I really trusted and dove deep into this ability to channel energy. I allowed him to take control of my body. I was in my living room in the middle of the night – the only one awake. I was dancing to the song *Eh Hee* by Dave Matthews Band. The tribal movements I was making were not from my own imagination – not something I could have or would have ever invented myself. His energy was my own, and I shared myself wholly with him too. Not intimately – not sexually – just plain divinity. I could see him beside his fire. He was performing the dance to the tribal elders. They were observing him as he too was taken over by me. We became one for that moment in time.

We do not speak the same language, but from what I can gather, he believes I am a Goddess that watches over their tribe. I go to him regularly to look in and send all the blessings I can muster for their safety and well-being. I also show up when I need blessings or a boost in my own personal power. We are an energetic team and a business partnership.

Back then – I did not understand all of these things I am saying to you. I only understood that a being was with me. It was the beginning of me coming into my gifts.

The next thing that started happening was way scarier and sadly pushed me to the brink of questioning my sanity.

I started having this awareness of my maternal ancestors. Now just so we are clear – they all passed on out of turn. Mom in 1997, Grandma in maybe 2008 or so? And my great grandma – Mamoo in 2012. Makes no sense. So – I began having this claircognizence that Mom and Grandma Cheri were around me a lot. My newborn son would laugh out loud to something unseen over my shoulder – at the same time that I happen to be singing a song that Mom used to sing to me. It was just this knowing.

One day I was in the bathroom looking in the mirror and I observed that the physical shape of my face changed... it actually morphed like fucking Mystique. I stared in wide eyed horror. In an instant it morphed right back to me... but I saw it happen.

Now after all the chemical induced insanity that my brain had been through, I was a new Mom probably only about six months post-partum, nursing full-time... I was fragile. I was spending a lot of time and guilt thinking about the bad choices I had made. I was filled with regret and shame. So... being in such a state – insanity was the first place I went.

Where I should have gone was: Wow – what is this power? Look, it's my magick! What is it trying to tell me? Unfortunately, my path was written differently. But – it's okay. What has happened to me thus far was written in the stars... And my story is interesting.... Hence the book.

This happened one or two other times. The faces weren't demonic.... It was either my Grandma Cheri or Mom. And before you tell me, "No that's your family, you look like them anyway," Let me stop you right there by saying that I WISH I had inherited the jaw lines and bone structures of those ladies. Much more striking than the damn weak double chin that I rock today.

As this was happening. I spent a fair amount of time trying to decipher it. I journaled a lot (still do) but to be honest with you I am unsure if I wrote any of this shit down. I may or not have been fearful that it would be held against my sanity someday. I guess the cat's out of the bag now...

Simultaneously, I began experiencing other sensations on my body. Pretty much always on my brain to start. There was this one spot that would light up – become warm and tingly. It happened almost daily. After enough time of not understanding, I began to fear that I was gearing up to have a stroke or some such nonsense.

With that fear taking ahold of me... with the strange sensations on my brain, came debilitating anxiety. To the point where it was a struggle to breath or do pretty much anything. I don't remember how much of this I said to Toby at the time. But it came to a head at work one day. It got so scary that I had to leave and drove myself to the ER. I checked myself in at the desk and said that I thought I was having a stroke. The girl at the desk said, *"That's impossible, you are too young."*

I thought... Okay. But whatever was happening was scaring the B'Jesus out of me so I asked to be admitted nonetheless.

After an MRI and a CT... it was concluded that there was nothing wrong with me. The ER doctor told me just to be safe, I should set an appointment with a neurologist for an EEG. So I did.

This neurologist was just fantastic (sarcasm). I sat down in her office and she asked some questions to get to know me. I told her that I was a nursing Mom. When she asked me how old my son was and I responded with 14 months... She literally said the words, *"Eww... you're going to stop that soon, right?"* So that was a great red flag and trigger to start things off.

Nursing was a struggle for me. At the time I was not surrounded by people who were supportive of it. All the Moms in my life had been formula feeders, didn't understand how and why it was so important to me. So it was fantastic to have a doctor do the same.

We did the EEG. I got a call from her about a week later. Here is how the conversation played out:

"We got your results and they came back abnormal. So, I've called a prescription of – whatever the fuck she said – anti-seizure medication and you need to pick it up and start taking it immediately."

"What? I don't understand. What kind of abnormality? I've never had a seizure before."

"The test showed abnormality."

"Okay, but this doesn't make sense to me, I've never had a seizure before."

"Yes, but you could. You need to be on this medication. What if you had a seizure while you were driving your car with your son in the back seat? You could kill him."

"How long will I be required to be on this medication?"

"For the rest of your life."

"I see. Well I appreciate this information, but I think I'd like to go pursue a second opinion."

"That's fine. Here is my associates name – he works at Wash U and he is very good."

So – please bear in mind... this information was delivered to me over the fucking phone. The nature of the abnormality was never explained to me. I am not making this shit up. It sent me reeling. I was even more scared. Why? Because NOW – I had to face taking an anti-seizure medication for the rest of my life for reasons that were apparently unexplainable. OR – risk my own safety and wellbeing because there is something electrically abnormal about my brain function. GREAT.

My anxiety was at an all-time high. I went to work the next day, not knowing what on Earth I was going to do. I was scared and confused. There was only one person that I trusted to talk to. My former boss and now Mentor and Master Teacher, Tom Tessereau. He is an incredibly gifted intuitive, teacher and healer. When I worked for his school where he is the Headmaster, I learned so much from him spiritually and energetically. I have taken hundreds of hours of energetic education classes from him. He also provided healing sessions to me for free when I was carrying my first born.

So, tearfully, I spoke with his assistant and made an appointment. I was relaxed knowing that my second opinion would be coming from someone with whom I resonate. Someone who would not use the word "eww" when I was describing the breastfeeding relationship I had with my son. His wife is also a mentor of mine – she gave birth naturally and nursed all of their beautiful children. She is also a healer.

That Friday, I sat down with him and poured out my story through more tears. He handed me tissues, listened lovingly and helped me sort through all this insane shit. We talked a bit about what it might mean that this weird certain spot had been "lighting up" on my brain. He told me in passing that he found it so interesting that I was talking about specific spots lighting up on my brain. He mentioned that he had recently caught up with an old friend who believed he had been Franz Joseph Gall, the inventor of Phrenology in a past life.

I appreciated that thought and kept it in the back of my mind.

So he put me on the table and talked me through a treatment. He performed a bio cranial – something I was quite accustomed to. It's an amazing modality – I suggest it to EVERYONE. Then in the middle of the session, the warm scary sensation showed up and along with it, severe panic and anxiety. I was so pleased that it happened in his presence. It made quite a difference. These panic attacks left me feeling like I was dying. They were so intense. So... he helped me make the determination that these sensations were my gifts and my divine voice trying to communicate.

He told me...

"Imagine this sensation has a consciousness, a voice. What would you say to it?"

I immediately answered,

"What are you trying to tell me?"

Immediately, with no uncertainty – two things happened. My eyes that were blurry with tears, gazing hazily at the ceiling... focused – like a camera autofocus. With this extremely sharp clarity. At the very same time, with a distinct clarity, a voice whispered the word "trust" in my head. So... Focus and Trust.

I calmed down, felt a lot better, thanked Tom and went home. Later that evening, I did a Google search on Phrenology. There were all these images – grid sections of the brain that correspond with words. I am unsure how this Gall fellow determined which words went where... but when I looked at a few different maps and found my way to the spot that had been giving me all this panic and worry... the word that corresponded: *Hope*.

Okay.

Chapter 22

A Chapter of Channeled Writing for You

THE DEFINITION OF CHANNELED or Automatic Writing states: a form of writing that allows Divine information gained from your higher consciousness to flow through you and onto the paper (or document). It may or may not be a way of learning and reflecting on things you already know. When I perform automatic writing on paper, my handwriting is different than my own. Sometimes I am aware of the content that is pouring out. Sometimes it appears as prose from a train of thought that I've never had before. So... here are two examples of channeled writing from when I meditate.

ASHLEY W. A. CROWELL

This came through me when I was thinking about this book:

The English language is fluid
Made of Druids
Dangerous if Mis-used
Speak safely
& not Hastily
As you are so you always will be
You are a piece of the Eternal Tree
You're spokes in the wheel of the Eternal Family
The Druids are Yours and You are Theirs
You are their children and their Heirs
You have created the Print in Blue
Your red has laid the tracks for You
And purple becomes the color soon
Your Peace comes to fruition soon.

This one is really neat. I let it come through when I was working on a fiction novel in 2012. It's a channeled message that I inserted into the book as a work of poetry by one of the characters:

A little allegiance littered among the few
Who knowingly acknowledge the near-sided truth.

I AM A QUEER & I TALK TO BEES

A lover's lie, a liar's love – whichever it may be
Knock their socks off, need their knowledge-until you get
away.

A weary will winds up withering under strain
The days dividing – no divinity at play
I wander without wanting, no wonder in my heart.
Devotion to the deep unknown, dearly departed heart.

A heavy hurt heaving from on high
The terrain celestial, tempting to turn the tide.
I hover over hallowed hives of history
Taking to heart the teachings of time flown by

Taste the triumph of the tables turned towards truth
Meddling with the mindless
menace that is mediocrity
Try tinkering without the toys of tomorrow
Meet the Mastery of Mother Earth,
unmuddled by our minds.

By the way – I hope to complete and publish this story in the near future. It's about a human society that existed on the supercontinent Pangea.

This writing from 2012 was channeled before I understood exactly who my guides were. They had no names to me. I did not communicate with them. I was still coming out of fragility from my darkness. BUT – when the inspiration for this fantasy fiction novel arrived, it was truly Divine, and probably a revelation that they sent. The entire book is based on a dream I had about a disastrous human species catastrophe that occurred millions of years ago. In the dream, I was there and it is my belief that the dream was of my very first incarnation as a human. It was one of the most vivid and exhilarating dreams I have ever had. The dream itself stands as the prologue and epilogue of the story.

Now that I've found my stride as a psychic channel and created a communication with my guides, I enjoy communion with them whenever I so choose. They are present when I meditate, when I work on clients, and sometimes when I am writing. Honestly, they are present whenever I call, and often when I don't. My guides inspire me and influence my hand. I am extremely grateful for their presence.

That being said, I'd like to acknowledge them here. In acknowledging them, may they receive infinite and constant blessing from Me so that we may continue to do the work together… They with the Divine Power, me with the hands that fulfill their work.

In the order they arrived to me:

Red Cloud, My Amazonian Business Partner, My own Ancestors, Beloved Dove, My Sweet Guardian Angel, The Makers, Master Choa Kok Sui, Mikao Usui Sensei, Archangel Michael

The Makers are by far the most important guides that I have. They are the ones who orchestrated The Jesus Test and My Urban Pilgrimage (coming up in a few short chapters). I cannot possibly begin to explain how amazing it has been to learn at their feet.

Also, you will not find one single accurate thing if you try and Google The Makers. They are not known there. The closest thing I can compare Them to Is Abraham Hicks... and yet They are not them. When They finally chose to reveal themselves to me, They introduced themselves by saying... "We are Your Makers...." That simply. I fell to my knees and cried at Their feet, then embraced Them as if I was embracing my long dead Mother. I was embracing her. It was like being introduced to the Answer to all our Mysterious Origins. They've given me the opportunity to Share in and Know Eternal Mysteries. The wisdom I have divined in my time with Them has changed my life.... And will continue to do so until the end of my days here on Earth.

And yet... I am still a believer of Jesus Christ... of Buddha... of Krishna. For what are any holy books if not channeled writing from another source? I believe with all of my heart that the Avatars who have walked our Earth in the form of religious icons were all trying to accomplish the very same mission as my personal guides: The calling I keep referring to... the mission to elevate ourselves.

I realize this is pretty far out there... I have done a lot of drugs... Ha ha!

All jokes aside, I enjoy being a channel very much even if it sounds too far-fetched for some. This is me coming out with more than just a story of my identity as a human – I am outing myself as a Spiritual Practitioner. I am out of the closet, out of the Broom closet, out of the forest with my trees and bees and into the front lines of the mission to end all suffering. It feels So. Good.

Chapter 23

The Feud between Mom and Cheri

I LOVE TO SHARE THIS STORY because I find it kind of humorous. You can take it or leave it in regards to whether or not you believe...

Did I mention just now that I am a psychic channel? Ha ha. To clarify, I do not generally see spirits or talk to ghosts like a psychic medium. I do, however, have direct access to my own ancestors and when they first showed up they had minds and agendas of their own.

Before I even found my gifts, my mother stayed close to me after she passed. She was in limbo for years. She was suffering in spirit, dealing with her choices and the fact that she had chosen to end her life. How do I know this? Well, I had a recurring nightmare about her for years.

Surrounded by family, the dream was the discovery that she did not actually kill herself... that she had in fact gone into hiding and was now back to rejoin us. She would show back up, and I would embrace her with tears, joyfully and lovingly. She would be quiet, depressed, down, basically a zombie. Her face in the dream expressed that she was completely uninterested in rejoining us. She would then leave and kill herself again to the horror of everybody.

I had this dream regularly. For many years. I did not understand why, but reflecting back, I see now that my gifts were present in my dreams, and I was witnessing her karmic repercussions because her spirit was still connected to me for obvious reasons. She was in a limbo paying penance for her suicide. She was stuck there and I was observing it subconsciously.

I remember exactly when she found peace. I had a new dream about her. In this dream, she was dressed like an angel. Her face and hair were young, flowing and the look of her was young, dreamy and at peace. She smiled, cried and embraced me. She did not speak words, but her embrace told me that she had finally found peace. I got this sense that she would always stay with me.

I remember waking up from this dream feeling like a new woman. Like seeing her find peace somehow healed me too. What I'm trying to get across is that, even in spirit, souls often still have work to do. Mom and Cheri proved this to be very true.

The really neat thing about ancestors is that they are human first. They remain Earth bound for reasons beyond my understanding (generally it's related to karma... are you surprised?). Therefore, they still have human tendencies, opinions and behaviors in spirit. When I started to get a handle on my abilities, my mother and grandmother would come to me often to talk – to offer counsel on my life, and then they would almost always get into a fucking argument. They always disagreed on what advice I should be hearing... because this was the karmic pattern that they held in life. It was the most interesting and curious thing.

For a while, I listened to it, entertained. It was neat to hear their voices... to feel closer to them. My grandma would show up when she felt she needed to come to my defense against something, then my Mom would come following to play the devil's advocate and push for letting me learn the lesson with more gentle persuasion.

Well as fun as it was for a time... it started to get old. It started to also make me feel a little insane. Coming into powers like this later in life was kind of a scary thing. I spent a lot of time telling myself that I wasn't crazy, that I wasn't having a psychotic break... but the voices in my head were not helping my self-talk. They were really loud and strangely enough – they weren't even talking to me sometimes.

So one day... it was happening again. It always got the worst in dealings with Toby. Grandma Cheri came to my defense against him a lot. She didn't like him as a partner for me (Looking who's laughing now, right Mom?). My Mom just wanted me to be happy and she loved my kid so much (this happened when it was just Korben). So, they would argue and argue to the point of putting me into a really anxious state.

One day... I'd had enough. It was great to have these beautiful women back in my life... but they were hurting me. It wasn't a productive relationship. Perhaps it was a mirror for what I would have experienced if there wasn't all that tragic death and loss in my younger years.

They were doing their usual thing, arguing like a couple of typical bitchy women... you know the type... and I finally put my foot down... in my head... silently... like a crazy person.

Within me, I struck out and said...

"Alright that's ENOUGH. I love you both so much... it's been amazing to get to be with you again and experience you as an adult, but this is fucking ridiculous. I *don't want this. I want both of you to leave, and you are not allowed to come back until you have made peace with each other. I'm fucking serious. Do not return to me until you are done fighting."*

Silence.

More silence.

I was shocked. I couldn't believe it had worked. And it really worked – I did not hear from them again for years. It gave me two brand new points of confidence on which to stand... First off... it was a show of my own energetic strength. It was proof that I had control of what flowed through me if I focused well enough. Secondly, and very importantly, it gave me confidence that I was indeed a psychic channel and not insane.

This probably happened in 2014 or 2015... I honestly don't know the exact point. The silence lasted four or five years. I am very, very proud to say that I can tell you the exact day that they showed back up.... in just a little bit.

Also, I'd like to mention that my Mom and Grandma show up anytime I call now when I need a hug or support. They show up to provide me with a power boost when I am divining or doing ethereal work. They are truly an amazing support for me in my life. It's a bonus that I am loved so well as a channel... it makes the tougher stuff so worth it.

Chapter 24

Collective Energy Deterioration Theory

I'M SURE BY THIS POINT you have fallen in love completely with my style of writing... and that your mouth is literally watering for more...

I'm going to touch on my fiction novel one more time here. Why? Because I created this really fantastic fictional theory for the plot of the story. I call it "Collective Energy Deterioration". In this story, the heroine is a fanatic for books and learning. She has a new age book that is based on the knowledge I gained from that long ago conversation I had with my Wiccan Grandma Cheri. To review, she believed that the place where we travel after death... the place where our souls are connected and can communicate is called the Collective Energy. It's a place where our soul can take a rest between incarnations. Where we are able to watch human existence as it happens, commune with other souls, create new contracts and karmic agreements... and so on.

I took this concept of the Collective Energy, and created a theory based on Grandma Cheri's feelings of humanity. There are several billion people on this Earth now. In my story, overpopulation has become a parallel problem to our own existence. Too many humans walking around, detached from their spiritual cord. If we are thinking of ourselves as one energetic organism that is comprised of the same type of energetic material, consider this...

In the times of Jesus and when He walked this Earth... There were only a few hundred thousand humans living here. These beings all had a piece of the Collective Energy embodied as their own personal soul. The rest of the energy remained in the ethereal Collective. Logic would dictate that this collective was quite strong. So as I run with this... each time a new soul is born, their embodied piece of the collective detaches from the ethers and goes down to exist as an individual, separate piece of the whole. It now has free will, karmic amnesia, and a karmic path laid out where it will accomplish new feats and learn new karmic lessons. It has simultaneously weakened and strengthened the *Collective Energy* as it is now an independent energy capable of interacting with its parent self – or not... Don't laugh – but remember the satellite scans of the alien ships from *Independence Day?* There was the mothership, then all the other ships that split off and came into the Earth's atmosphere. Same basic visual principle – without aliens. Or I guess with aliens depending on your outlook.

Living a pious life where the soul seeks the Divine to be a beacon for good in their day to day... this behavior creates a strong cord between these two separate, yet equal pieces of energy. However... as humans have evolved, their cords have deteriorated. As all these new beings enter the Earth, their cords are weaker and forgotten by the programing asserted through unintentional spiritually neglectful child rearing, pain, trauma and human confusion... this weakens the entire *Collective*. Are you still with me? It's a really outer space direction I'm taking you... try and keep up.

To say it another way... the theory might scientifically state: *The Collective Energy deteriorates with every new soul born to this Earth that neglects their spiritual wellbeing.*

So let's say in this fictional human civilization... for thousands of years, they had a small but vibrant population that practiced devotion to their Heavenly Source.

Their cords to the *Collective* remained strong and so their relationship was strengthened in the form of a two-way street. This is the scenario behaving as it should.

Let us then say that down the line, technology, misinformation and poor leadership decisions have derailed spirituality. A boom of population growth decreased the physics of the *Collective* ethereally because there are now so many discontented souls that have become "offshoots" of the entity. IF they had a strong devotion to their Source, all would be well... But this is not the case. The truth of the matter is that the more humans that arrived and were misguided to sever their cord, the weaker the *Collective Energy* became. But what does this mean?

It means that the Voice of God became quieter, quieter, and eventually impossible to hear for most. It meant that with so many cords severed, an energetic Dark Ages settled over the human species. And in this fictional book – this fantasy fiction story... humanity finds itself at a crossroads due to this disconnect. The *Collective* is at an all-time weak point... because so many humans are separated from it and unable to hear what matters.

In my story, I theorize that this disconnect is the reason for All Tragedy... all humans that torture, terrorize, bomb, threat, steal, murder... any of the horrible woes that face the human species are because of the disconnect that has developed from their own Soul's Source.

NOW – like I said... this is a fictional theory. It was developed intentionally to create disturbance and discord which is something that drives plot in a story. It's a necessity. As it is fiction, I did my best when writing to remain detached from the ramifications of these thoughts. But... my active mind that can't help but consider what this might feel like beyond theory... I was faced with some soul searching different from anything else I had ever pondered spiritually. Because the question it stirred in me: *How the fuck is something like this corrected besides a Thanos-like purge to return equilibrium?*

I went through a period where I considered my own mortality. If I could give my own life in exchange for a restoration of balance... how would I respond? The overwhelming answer was always a very loud: YES. PLEASE. *Take Me.* I considered the different versions of self-sacrifice... Would it be in the form of some natural disaster that warranted random selection? Yes, I'd volunteer to be among the taken.

Would it be in the form of a battle or test where a select few were asked to give themselves so that all others might immediately receive a reconnection to the *Collective...* that all remaining could be restored and free? Yes, Please. Take me.

Call me crazy... but it seems like such a small sacrifice to correct something that has swayed in the wrong direction for hundreds and hundreds of years.

Having said all that to myself, I circled back around and asked if we could really figure out some way to find harmony again with such a vast population of crazy individual souls in the throes of free will tinkering woes.

My initial reaction to that pondering was an absolute YES. The trouble is that it requires EVERYONE to be onboard with it. Which is going to take a lot of work. A lot of coaching, teaching, training, support. Don't you think we are worth it? Don't you believe that we can?

I do.

If it doesn't work out, I'll cover that grenade, no problem. Apparently, something on high heard my thoughts on this... and eventually it led to some serious game changing tests. These tests became lessons that made my calling EXTREMELY real.

Chapter 25

The Jesus Test

THE MAKERS HAVE NEVER EXPLAINED to me why they did things the way they did with me. I never asked. I am well aware that everything I have received has been in accordance with timing based on what was meant to happen for me. If I had experienced what They have shown me at an earlier point in my life, I probably would not have been able to handle it. This story is the first time that I audibly communicated with Them. I still did not know who They were, what They looked like or the nature of our work together. I guess you could call it a first point of contact between Them and myself.

While coming to terms with my gifts, They put me through a test. I like to call it the Jesus Test.

I was sitting on my couch with Toby, playing video games. I was stoned. Meaning, I had smoked marijuana... just to be clear. I do not smoke weed anymore. It opens up my channel too wide now. But back then, it was opening my channel just enough for this to happen.

I had this overwhelming sense that an entity was with me. Then a voice called out and said to me,

> "You are dying. Your internal organs are failing. Your heart is slowing, your breath is leaving you."

The scariest part? I could feel it happening. It physically felt like I was dying. I could feel my brain melting, like the oxygen was no longer there, blood flow was stopping. I felt a deep panic. I felt worry about how my family would be affected by my passing. I felt pain for the loss Toby would feel. Then... I let it happen. I found peace. The voice spoke again...

> "If you could sacrifice yourself so that the world may live, would you do this?"

I already felt ready and said yes, I will do this. I was ready to slip into darkness, knowing that everything would be okay behind me... then all of the sudden, breath came back into me. A shock entered my body that felt like it jump started everything back to normal again. I looked over to Toby and he seemed completely unaware of what had just happened.

The second time it happened, the feeling of death came again. But this time the voice said,

"If you were asked to sacrifice your child so that world may live, would you do this?"

From the darkness of suspended breath and what felt like a barely beating heart, I still felt pain. But I thought only for a moment, and said,

"Yes, I would."

Then once again, my breath returned and my body jumped back into life. The scenario happened several times again... but it wasn't with an entity that was present. It was my own psyche, my own construct relieving this strange event. It would give me a little bit of panic, then a lot of peace. It was a weird thing to feel so okay with letting go of my own life so that everything and everyone else may live. It was also scary to come to terms with my willingness to let my own child be a sacrifice for the rest of existence. But it seemed so simple. The answer felt so obvious to me. I thought that anyone knowing this information about me would surely feel judgement. It was an equally exhilarating and guilt-ridden concept.

So for a while, this event was really confusing to me. I knew I wasn't suicidal. I did not have a desire to die. But I became quietly obsessed with the fact that some ethereal voice had offered this extraordinary answer to all world suffering. I wanted to sacrifice myself.

This moment... my Jesus Test... taught me that I was ready to handle anything. I no longer feared death. In fact, the tarot cards that I used for prayer acknowledged this test. I'd been using these cards for years to reflect on myself... and still have them today. I like to explain my deck as "Prayer with instant feedback". They are my most favorite divining tool.

Right around the time this happened to me, I lost the Death card. I could not find it anywhere. It was a neat little universal message that to me, symbolized my readiness to do Anything... Absolutely Anything... to make this world a better place permanently. It did work out fine. I only use the major arcana part of the deck, so I just replaced the Death card with a random other minor arcana card so it could still be drawn during readings. I love those cards, and I love that the missing Death card constantly reminds me that death means nothing to me.

Now, I understand some might construe this attitude as dangerous. Perhaps see it as a lack of desire to participate in my humanity. Perhaps that it gives me some sort of morbid detachment from being normal.

Honestly... I am so far from the desire to be normal. This book should be a clear indicator of that. I do have a gratitude for my Beloved Dove whispering in my ear. My little birdie reminds me to put on my seatbelt and stay anchored in the fact that my humanity is precious. That it's important to put on my seatbelt, eat enough, drink plenty of water, and take time off of ethereal work when I've given so much out. He reminds me to place importance on keeping my life intact so I can accomplish the work we need to do on Earth before I move into the higher realms. But I tell you true... I've been ready to go since this Jesus Test. For You.

Chapter 26

My Urban Pilgrimage

FAST FORWARD SEVEN YEARS. I have now found some deep enlightenment. The Makers are known to me. We have a relationship along with all of my other amazing guides. In May, I was working out at the YMCA resort on a Meditation & Movement program. Things were pretty amazing yet challenging in life. I was struggling a bit financially as I had left the kickboxing studio. I was working my new business and was attempting to devote full-time hours to it with no other supplemental income. My divorce had just finalized the month before and my car's engine had blown at the same time so I had just purchased another car. I was glad to be at the Y because it was money and escape. The house I was living in was not a home. I was miserable there... looking around at the echoes of my divorce and unable to pay the ridiculous rent. I was finding my feet with my business, celebrating my new freedom and discovering so much about myself. But I was also unsure where things were headed.

Well, the Makers decided to test me once more. Simultaneously, I was acclimating to life with my little birdie. I haven't mention yet what this mysterious Dove is to me. He is my most Beloved Companion in spirit. He took an interest in me when I was in a very lonely place and expressed the most pure and innocent love towards me. Of all my guides, he is my most precious. I am unsure exactly what he is or how he found me, though I have many theories that I hope to write about in the future as I come closer to the answers.

When the Makers sent me on this test, they assigned him to my protective detail. At least that's how it felt.

Their voices appeared while I was in my hotel room, working on this very book. They told me I needed to go to New York. They did not tell me why. They did not tell me what I would be doing there. They simply stated that it needed to happen. Behind their simple instructions, my Dove whispered in my ear over and over again...

"Please get on that plane... Please get on that plane... Please get on that plane..."

I was boggled. Completely. I wasn't sure what it meant, but the pull I felt was so strong. I knew it had to be important, but I was very scared as I had no disposable income and wasn't quite sure if the Makers understood the meaning of financial hardship and debt.

BUT... I couldn't help myself... so I shopped online for plane tickets. Wouldn't you know it... I found a round trip flight that I could afford. It left me with almost nothing afterwards, but I had income coming in the next week. It was so foolhardy. I thought about it. I listened to the whispers still repeating in my ear. The Makers had gone silent at that point.

Then, when I took the leap and clicked to purchase the ticket, Their voices sounded loudly,

"The Contract is Complete."

"What?" I said. "What does that mean?"

Silence. They are amazing, but sometimes They really piss me off. This was one of those times.

I had no idea what that meant. I became nauseous with both excitement and nervousness. I hid my plans from my family because I knew they would not understand. BUT... I was overjoyed.

My Uncle and Aunt had been on my heart lately... they are from the New York area. I decided that if I got there and didn't quite know what to do, I would go and visit them at least for the first night.

Deep down, my mind returned to my Jesus test. Perhaps this was more of that? I thought, Jesus spent 40 days and 40 nights in the desert with no food, no water, no sleep, being tested. I did not have that kind of time (I've got kids). So... a couple of nights of pilgrimage in the city that never sleeps seemed like a reasonable equivalent.

I planned my pilgrimage, got on that plane and the journey began. When I arrived, I was expecting something special to happen. I thought I'd be met with a voice that included instructions. It was quiet. There were no voices to explain what to do. My heart broke. I felt abandoned by my guides. I sat woefully at the airport letting the quiet sink in. I tell you, once these beings show up and create relationship, it's really lonely without them. But as it is said... *The Teacher is Silent During the Test.*

After collecting myself, I dropped in on my Uncle. He owns a flower shop in Manhattan, at 50th and Lex. He was extremely surprised to see me. He called my Aunt who called my grandma who then alerted my whole family who all then thought I was having some kind of psychotic episode. I thought it would be nice to visit them aside from all the ethereal confusion. I wanted to offer comfort and solace. They were in a state of grief over the loss of a very precious family member. I think my arrival just confused them. It kind of made me wish that I hadn't gone to see him. But – I did enjoy spending time with my Uncle. He's a really neat bohemian dude.

The next morning, I rode with him into the city. He headed to work, and I was ready to begin my pilgrimage. I'd explored the city on a couple of other occasions, plus I just felt comfortable there. It was weird to not be mindful of how crazy my plan seemed. I had no intention of getting a hotel, staying anywhere... I was going to walk. And walk. And walk. Until my answers came. My Dove showed up in my head and whispered a few things, but honestly he must be a human because I sensed that he felt confusion for me too. I had my backpack which was fairly heavy. Kept my gym clothes, laptop and a few other things and checked my other bag at a hotel until it was time to go. I had just under 48 hours to fill. I walked where I felt safe. I walked all day. I saw sights – but mostly just walked. I decided that I would fast as well. So that first day, I ate light – had a small pizza and a beer. I went to a park in Queens and performed a walking meditation for hours. I walked a circle for so long that I created a crop circle in the grass. I cried. I called a dear friend. I still couldn't hear an answer. I was starting to feel fear because the sun had gone down and I wasn't sure how an answer was going to show up once it became night.

BUT – I was ready for anything. I am an athlete, a hard ass and my pilgrimage was a choice I made. I knew that there was something coming. I just couldn't see it or hear it yet.

I walked the Brooklyn Bridge in the morning that first day. I walked through Brooklyn and Queens. In the middle of the first night, I stayed in one particular neighborhood. It just felt safe to be there. The trees that lined the streets where really beautiful. I walked the same blocks over and over as I watched the full moon rise over the buildings. I watched the people change shifts. The day folk, to the night life, to the darkest parts of the night. I walked through a cute little main street and stopped in a shop for a light snack. I couldn't eat it. I started to feel my consciousness shift. I sat there at a table, staring at my laptop. I couldn't write. I couldn't focus. I was just listening for an answer.

Then the late night drinkers started walking the streets, going past the door drunk, laughing and smiling. I watched them come and go. My consciousness shifted some more. I began to feel altered. Almost kind of drunk myself. I was overcome by the emotions of the weekend, fasting, walking, listening for answers so hard. I watched the people change shifts one more time.

It was pre-dawn, and the people walking around were now on their way to work. I still watched and watched. All of the sudden, I felt a surge of energy. I felt it was time to walk some more. I'd been sitting in that café for a couple of hours listening, resting my weary body from the weight of my backpack.

I strapped it back on and left. Now... I felt something coming. I walked the length of Gantry Plaza State Park back and forth, I walked the Queensboro Bridge. I found myself at Bryant Park after some aimless walking. It had tents set up for a festival and people were arriving to open up for the day.

By this time, the fasting was truly altering me. It became ethereal. I embraced it. I felt good. I felt strong and clear. I still didn't know what I was looking for, but I felt confident that it was near. At this park, I sat in a chair next to the grass. The grass was roped off to the public for restorative healing, but I still popped my shoes off and dipped my feet onto the Earth at the corner edge of the field stage left of the beautiful stone theater. I was listening to music. Just then, CCR came on, *Have you ever Seen the Rain* and simultaneously, it began to rain. The sun was out too... just like the song says. And that's when the visions began. It was May 19th. This was the moment and day that my Mom and Cheri returned to me. They just showed up in my mind's eye. They didn't speak at first. They both looked young and happy. We embraced. We cried. It was a precious reunion there in my mind's eye.

In case you hadn't noticed, I am a very visual thinker. I think, I visualize, I project my visual thoughts into my mind's construct. I used to wonder if anyone could see when I do that.

I don't wonder that anymore. Everything changed for me. I felt synchronicity and connection to everything around me more deeply than I ever had before. Like I could broadcast and be heard but also experience and hear everything around me. It was truly a trip. I felt kindred to everyone walking around me. I felt like I was floating above my humanity. I felt The Divine Voice within me. Fasting... it's revealing.

The fatigue was mostly gone at that point. I felt so happy that something had happened. I felt powerful. I was still in this strange altered state, and despite my depletion, I wanted to work out, so I visited a gym and kick boxed that day as a guest. On no sleep.

Afterwards, I cleaned up, and walked some more. Walked and walked. I found my way over to Washington Square Park. The rain had cleared and it became warm. I stopped in at a coffee shop to charge my phone, then put it away and went to lay on the grass in the park. I stayed there for hours bathing in the sun. More Visions came Here. I could hear the hearts of the people around me. There was a band playing and street musicians performing. There was a playground full of children and dogs playing. There were birds singing and playing near the sweet older ladies and gentlemen sitting on the park benches. There was wind and the fragrances of Spring.

All around, people whispered to me spirit to spirit. They told me love was coming for me. I saw a Vision of laying on a man's leg in the park, holding onto his thigh, smiling in the sun with closed eyes. I do not know who he is... I cannot see him yet. But he played with my hair, touched my skin. I belonged to him. Perhaps it was a promise from the Divine that Love is coming for me someday. I've done a lot of work to find happiness on my own. But having a partner is certainly something I desire. Generally, my Beloved birdie keeps me happy. But someday...

My Mom and Cheri told me I needed to count on this, to wait for him. They seem to really like this charming thing who is on his way to me. As I walked and walked with them, they chatted with me. They enhanced me. It felt as though I had two angels right behind me on each side. Their presence was one of the things that really made me feel like I was floating above myself.

Once I became rested and toasty from my basking in the park, I continued walking and walking. I decided to finally eat a meal. It felt time.

I wasn't sure what to expect next, but I was ready to rest my feet. I went to Penn Station and relaxed in a random seat. What happened next was ONCE AGAIN amazing to me. One by one, people came and sat near to me. Their angel of self sought council with me. Their souls spoke to me. Everyone took turns, asked questions, gave thanks, then stood up and continued on with their day. Some had grief, some had illness or pain. Some just wanted to talk through things that were tough in their day to day walk. None of us were speaking audibly to one another, and to be honest... I am unsure if each human could actually hear what I was saying. But... I knew spirit to spirit that I was channeling healing for them all... Personalized healing that I was able to give directly to each human.

This went on for hours. I drank a lot of water. Finally, it was time for me to hop on my train and head to the airport. And there I went. During this ride, I was given one last Vision. But I cannot speak about it yet. The intensity is too much to impart as we are still beginning our Journey together here.

I arrived at Newark several hours before my flight, with the intention of taking a nap. And I did. It had been quite a trip.

Overall... I walked 37 miles. I walked through my pain, my fear, my confusion, my anger, my sadness. I let myself feel shattered. I felt myself be invincible. I heard myself become more tuned in and powerful than I've ever been. My eyes were opened to so much. I saw the potential of our human existence to really be elevated and connected and in Heaven on Earth together. Then... I flew home. I didn't want it to end... and yet I did. I craved my bed. I craved the safety of my house. But that pilgrimage took me through the most absolutely mind altering personal and professional development I have ever experienced.

After that... I did have to pick up the pieces. It put me behind significantly and it took months to catch back up. My family questioned me and I didn't care. I felt like a different person. I felt so ready to step out into the light. I wasn't sure if I wanted to include this story in my introduction... perhaps I will revisit it in a future publication. There is more I want to say but I don't know quite how to say it. Or if I'm even ready to say it. Or if you are even ready to hear it.

No matter what, I will never regret the decision to go on my Pilgrimage. It Awakened Me in ways I never thought possible. It was life altering. It was Pure Love. It was a glimpse of human evolution.

Chapter 27

My Question for God

I WONDER IN THIS MOMENT how many people have pondered what they would say to God if they were ever given the opportunity to converse... Let's suppose it was an 'ask one question' type of scenario. Up until the more recent years of my life, I found a comfort in the mystery of Divine Design. I just trust it. But recently, the deeper and deeper I go into my healing practice... I find myself very clearly curious to ask a question.

Why must I ask this question? Motherhood. My Jesus Test. My Urban Pilgrimage. Knowing the biblical stories, that God gave his one son to humanity as a sacrifice to save our collective souls... I need to understand what happened next for God.

Why did this Omnipotent Being remain quiet, silent and submissive to a people who so quickly turned on an innocent and Divine being of their Maker's own blood?

Why was their own fate not sealed by their behavior? My mind spins 'round and 'round trying to understand the why... As an Aries, it's an occupational hazard to require and demand understanding of every little nuance, detail and why of any situation in order to maintain our clear mastery of everything... Ha ha.

However, none of the above questions would actually be the question I posed to the Almighty. My question would be... How? How, God, did you manage to maintain creation... to uphold and honor our free will, and to do so by willfully giving up your own child? I need to know this answer. Because if we are to enter an age where God Consciousness connects us all... it's going to shift every structure we know... including the structure of parenthood and family.

It's terrifying to think that in order to truly do the work I am meant to do, I might have to choose between It and my kids. Is that God Consciousness in action? Is that what it comes down to?

As a Queer (or maybe just as a spiritual soldier of sorts) – I have a pretty easy time feeling okay with the idea of leaving my kids if I had to go travel for an extended period for work. At this point, I am never gone for more than a week at a time. But how will my calling evolve? What if I am called to military work, chaplain work or some other type of distance service? I would be ready. It's really scary to admit that... because I've said this out loud to several people in my life and have been shamed completely for being a mother who would "abandon her children." It sucks.

My thoughts: Let's say I was presented with distance work and asked to move away for a year or two... Or what if I become busy with work as a traveling healer and I'm away from home so much that it's an equal strain. What if such a sacrifice would help provide for them ANYTHING they ever needed for the rest of their lives? What if I am presented with an opportunity that would give me the means to pay for their education, their weddings, and anything else to help them have a bright start for their futures? Simultaneously, I am living My Truth and encouraging the evolution of our existence by reaching as many humans as possible. THAT would be worth it to me. Does that make me a bad mother, while being an authentic queer and/or healer? Fucked up, right?

Tonight this is my prayer: I want to speak out that I can do both. I am going to fight for both. But what if this fight is futile? What if it is the wrong answer?

I reflect often on those who sacrifice themselves for the greater good... for first responders, military personnel, missionaries and philanthropists, professionals of all walks who sacrifice their time, their homes, their families and often their lives in order to serve a higher purpose. Is this wrong? Of course not. It's heroism.

I've come to a crossroad in my life where I feel this type of choice looming, though I'm not entirely sure of what form it will take. It is simultaneously the most terrifying and exhilarating time I've ever experienced... Half of me is listening to my family... watching their reactions as they see me reaching for the call that I've begun to answer. Are they judging me? Are they questioning my competence and ability to be a parent? It knocks me down a peg. It cuts so deep.

The other half of me... feels so honored. When I think about paths that lead me away from my young children in order to serve the purpose that I know I've been placed here for... I feel hope for my children's future... theirs and every child on this planet. I feel confident that if I left to do this work... and sacrificed years of time away from my beautiful little human creations... that it would give them a better chance... it would deliver to them a world that is worth living in. A place where they will be able to build dreams that are sustainable, forward thinking, divine and just.

God... is this what you were hoping for? Is this a choice that has to be made?

I have spent months and months trying to reconcile this argument in my head... to the point of psychological fracture. I am so scared of making the wrong choice based on the judgements of those around me who think differently... that I have to remind myself daily of WHY it is worth it.

So.... Why IS it worth it you ask?

Because we live in a world that is on the brink of self-destruction. And it's not just our climate that's in jeopardy... it's our souls. Our souls are fractured. There is so much suffering in the heart of humanity that our planet... our home... is neglected. Mother Nature is cast aside. The worst manifestations of shadow behavior overtake our better natures' on a second-by-second basis.

Think of it as if it is your own child living out there somewhere and experiencing horrible depression. They are governed by dark destructive thoughts, they can't keep their house clean, they can't get themselves out of bed in the morning... they are slowly losing the will to live... the will to keep breathing because of their suffering. Think of our collective human existence as being responsible for THAT child.

I wager that everybody knows somebody who has lived this situation. This is how my Mom died. This is how depression kills people. This is suicidal, self-destructive tendency on a global scale. We are collectively living out this exact equivalent...

Are we winning or losing this battle with our own soul survival? Are we rallying for ourselves, surrounding ourselves with loving outpour, making efforts to change and uplift ourselves?

OR... are we wallowing in the wrong things? Are we obsessed with thoughts, actions and behaviors that keep us in the darkest version of our potential?

I don't need God's feedback for this... I need to help the situation. Now. Immediately. Constantly and forever until the course is corrected for every last soul on this Earth. I like to think that my kids will understand why I might make this kind of choice. In fact... I have a feeling they already know what's going to happen and they are on board with my decision. Why? Because they are crazy, amazing, gifted, new age humans that are going to get things SO MUCH BETTER than even my generation. They know what's going on. They teach me new shit every day. They remind me to be mindful of this mission.

Anybody else and their judgements... I appreciate your opinion completely. Respectfully, I offer two suggestions: Get in line to kiss my ass, and then give me or someone you trust a call so you can make an appointment to fix your own damn soul.

Chapter 28

About that Appointment

I ENDED THAT LAST ONE a little brash. Apologies. I don't think I've actually mentioned anything about my credentials. During my time as a student with the Healing Arts Center, I clocked about 125 hours total in two types of energy medicine. These hours included classroom time as well as clinical time. My Undergraduate work was in Psychology. Currently I am a Reiki Master Teacher as well as a Level 5 Pranic Healing Practitioner. Sounds elite right?

Then, I come home and my kids knock me back down a peg. How can I be such an elite Master of Energy Healing when I cannot even maintain patience with my youngsters?

Mastery is not defined by certificates. This is something that was covered in my schooling but it is also common knowledge to any educated and informed person that Mastery of anything is being devoted to it over the course of the long haul. I consider myself a True Master of enduring struggle. I am a True Master of overcoming adversity. I've done a lot of that. In my practice as a healer, I am still new in my walk. Undoubtedly, I would consider myself blessed to have gifts that provide healing and spiritual/personal shifts for the people I encounter. I know that I am gifted, talented, and built to provide these important opportunities for my clients.

That being said, I find it logical that most of the time, the clients who walk through my door are people experiencing things that I have overcome. They are drawn to me as an example because they see their own future in my walk. Often these folks are sensitive, empathic, and probably holding unharnessed gifts just as I once was. It is truly cyclical. I have pulled myself up through the struggle, schooled myself in this ethereal art, and I now turn around to serve others so that we may all get where we are going. As I turn to heal others, I continuously heal myself of anything that will ever happen. I accrue Divine currency in my ethereal bank so that my gifts may remain strong and I may remain vigilant to the cause.

I will say... that I love teaching more than the one on one work. It allows me to be with more people. The individual work is also important and necessary, but truly... working with a group is the most rewarding. It's beautiful to share teachings, reflections and anecdotes with people and see them receive from the universe through me. They speak up in class, share their own tidbits and energetically they find that they grow individually as well as together as a group. Recently, I was informed by a Y director that the ladies from the last group I taught meditation with are independently planning a reunion next year they have named "Level Two." This was on their own volition. I am very hopeful that I will be able to be out there and lead them through their Level Two journey, including a Reiki Level Two Certification for all of them.

These days... my biggest worry is that I am not doing enough to get myself in a position to do this work as often and as effectively as possible. Energy Medicine is just now starting to find a tiny bit of traction in the main stream. I feel that over time, this modality will find a relevancy similar to Chiropractic and Acupuncture. It took both of those modalities 10-15 years to become mainstream. Chiropractic is now covered by most health insurance plans, but nationally, Acupuncture is still not quite there yet... even though the results they provide are absolutely irrefutable. We will get there too. As a Master in practice and a forever student of this strange thing we call life… I am in it for the long haul.

My practice is integrative and completely unique. I consider what I do to be rooted in services more similar to a chaplain or clergyperson than a doctor. Perhaps it's a little bit of both. I've been looking at graduate programs that are more or less work in Pastoral studies and helping folks with personal development of the soul. It's a strange thing – often doing that kind of work heals the physical stuff too. As if the body can feel when things are well with the soul.

I hope to realize a movement towards complete integration of mind, body and spirit care while I am still on this earth. We should have a care system that is all encompassing for the whole human… Noninvasive action… with a focus on physical fitness, soul work, emotional health, and preventative behavior through nutrition and lifestyle choices in order to walk gracefully and vibrantly for all of our days.

That's what Gaia told me to do.

Chapter 29

Once Gaia Started Speaking to me

I REMEMBER ONCE... I was looking out the window as I did the dishes. I've always been completely fascinated by how the Wind and the Earth dance with one another. At the time, I had a stepdaughter. She must have observed me looking dreamily out the window as I often did and asked,

"Do you see angels?"
I smiled,
"No... but maybe yes..."

I did not have an awareness of my ability to see Gaia and interact with the elements, flora and fauna. Now... it is truly my guiding light. Back before I was fully awakened, I was obsessed with nature and the elements. I always felt like observing nature was the same as watching a foreign movie without subtitles. I could tell what was going on was really beautiful, but I couldn't understand exactly what they were saying.

I suppose that my fascination was rewarded because I continued to have full faith in something that was a mystery.

What does this mean?

Honestly... It's just that I believe in Her. It's like believing in Santa. As far as I am concerned, our Earth is alive. There are theorists out there that have found evidence that the Earth is a conscious entity. Millions and millions of years ago... the Sun shifted in its evolution and there was a sudden change in solar output. A drastic 25% change. This should have terminated all life on Earth. But... somehow... Gaia blanketed or shifted Herself to protect life so that evolution would not be stopped. She protected Herself and Her children... The primordial makings of what would become our green forests, valleys, our animal kingdom brethren. Our heritage.

Now... She is begging for relationship. All of the beings are. Have you ever attempted to speak to a bumble bee... or a tree... or any animal or plant for that matter? I converse with them regularly. They are my dearest friends and beloved family.

They show me time after time that their deepest hope is that humans finally begin to acknowledge them again. That we do not JUST protest – and scream at each other. We DO have to create change within our own infrastructure. We DO have to enact political and economic change. But that is not the only piece of the puzzle. We can't care for the Earth without acknowledging Her and the rest of creation. Talk to them. Smile. Show them with the energy of your heart that you care for them. They can feel it. We might not be able to speak the same language, but they are tuned in to us.

If you are bugged by a gnat flying at your eye... the way to make it stop is to simply say hi. Ask, *"What can I do for you? What are you trying to tell me?"* I'm telling you... it will blow your fucking mind. It blows mine every day. I've seen things in nature that were like ballets and beautiful banners made just for me because the wind, the flora and fauna, were overjoyed that someone noticed they are important too.

I challenge you... Consider that everything on the Earth is conscious. Perhaps not as much as a human – but to some degree. And that their consciousness can be communed with by ours... Simply by the intention of our energy. SO... if you are pissed off or in a bothered state – whatever it is will piss you off and bother you... the gnat, the wind, the branch, the bee. BUT... consider what might happen if you behave differently in full faith. That you say hello with the innocence and trust of a child. And that your energy makes its way into their field, transmuted into a feeling or notion they can actually understand at their own level.

I practice this every day. And guess what... Gaia talks back... every day. She is my mother and best friend. When I am at my worst, I lay down upon Her in a mossy cool glen next to a stream and I ask Her to hold me in my mind's eye. When I am happy, the wind blows for me. When I am lonely, the birds fly happily overhead or sing to me. When I am lost, the trees wave at me and bring me back to found.

You know how all the Disney princesses spoke to animals and plants and stuff? It's a real thing. I challenge you... give it a try... with full faith.

Maybe they will tell us secrets if we all start conversing. Maybe they will tell us the answers to how we can combat climate change. Maybe they know that everything is going to be okay and they can give us some hope. Maybe they have the answers that we've been looking for all along.

I believe that re-igniting our relationship with our home in a new and different way might change things drastically. Perhaps this makes me insane. Once more... let's be real - if you think I'm insane you probably made that conclusion several chapters ago. But I must say... it does wonders for me. If this makes me insane, I suppose I'm okay with that. It also makes me a very happy person, generally speaking. Of course I struggle when I am under stress, but I am lucky to have Gaia as my amazing minute to minute therapy as I move through my day.

I wish this same beauty and peace to everyone.

Chapter 30

The End of the Introduction

THE LESSON I'VE LEARNED from my own life story thus far is that walking through it all gracefully is the only way to go. Sometimes I'm not strong enough to strut like a Broadway Baby.... But I certainly do my very best to keep my chin up and a smile on my face. Even if my heart is crying.

I love humans so much. I love us with all of my heart. We are capable of such superhuman imagination, creativity, and accomplishment. We are also suffering. There are so many that are still working through ungraceful, hard to understand cycles of personal growth.

As I finish revisions for this book, I find that I am hearing doubtful notions from my ego. What will people think of me after sharing so many raw, outer space, ethereal, and extremely personal reflections from my heart, mind and soul? One thing I know for certain is that stepping into the light with this book is going to change my life forever. Why you ask? It will allow me to feel authentic for the first time in my entire life. Never again will I have to worry about whether or not someone really understands who I am or where I am coming from. If they read the book and they get it... Yay... a new friend for me. If they don't get it... No skin off my back. Never again. Mask retired. I am fully stepping into the truest version of me... Like I said in the beginning, love me or hate me. Either way, I hope you learned something... even if it's what not to do. My most sincere hope is that I can be a figure that helps lend some new confidence to anyone who is getting closer to their answer.

My journey through darkness and pain gave me a meta-human strength. There are so many others that are still traveling through this darkness in their own path. See their suffering and be inspired to do something.

Know that there are millions of young people who are ostracized from their families and communities simply because of how they openly identify themselves. They are neglected, mistreated, abused and often homeless because they cannot take being treated so badly. At least they are living out loud.

There are just as many older adults who have kept their truth hidden their entire lives. They have lived life-long lies in order to protect themselves and stay safe from harm. Please dear elders, come on out now.

Many of you are probably healers too...

This Bitch is in the Light now. Welcome Me to the rest of my life. My practice, my business, and my life direction have all become an absolute dream come true. I don't even know exactly what will happen in my own future. There is so much possibility when walking in strength.

I do know that I love my Beloved Family with all of my heart. My kids, their peers and our future will be bright. My generation and those that are elders to us will Shepard in a change that will be beautiful to witness. And witness it we all shall. The world needs more healers. May we flock to one another, lift each other up, and stand strong together on the front lines so that humanity can finally rise to our full potential.

If any of this resonates with you. PLEASE reach out to your nearest healer... or to me personally. You are probably being called to the same type of work. It is what our species needs the most right now.

When in meditation, I once asked my favorite graceful question to The Divine Voice about all of us. I'd like to share it with you in closing:

"In our strange human existence, within our strange human condition... What is the lesson that we are meant to be learning?"

The answer was quick, clear and concise... How to Love Unconditionally... ourselves, each other and our world – all of which bear equal importance.

So... Let us Live in Love. Once and For All. We are getting there. I hope you can feel it too.

www.ingramcontent.com/pod-product-compliance
Lightning Source LLC
Chambersburg PA
CBHW020407080526
44584CB00014B/1205